A Man of a Few More Words

More Short Humour by Swan Morrison

Includes the songs of Swan Morrison
with guitar chords

Copyright © 2010 by Swan Morrison

ISBN: 978-1-4092-9664-5

This book is dedicated to:
Alan, Bob and Robin, who continue to be a greater inspiration to me than they probably realise;
Philippa, who very generously agreed to proofread this book,
and
Linda, who I love very much.

A Man of a Few More Words

Welcome to the World of Short Humour!!

Short Humour is any kind of humorous writing of around 500 words. This book is full of it.

Before we carry on with the comedy, however, may we have your attention for a few further words of explanation?

In 2006, Swan Morrison published *A Man of Few Words*, a collection of one hundred examples of Swan's Short Humour with a connecting theme of life in the modern world.

This book is a second such collection and includes one hundred further comedy stories, dialogues, poems, letters, spoof news reports, articles and songs.

Also in 2006, *the Short Humour Site* was created at *www.short-humour.org.uk*. This site continues to promote the reading and writing of Short Humour, both in Britain and throughout the world. *The Writers' Showcase* on the Site now includes hundreds of pieces by numerous writers. Two anthologies of work from *the Writers' Showcase*, *People of Few Words* and *People of Few Words – Volume 2*, have been published in print, and further volumes are planned.

All profits from the sale of work by Swan Morrison are currently donated to a UK registered charity supporting people in Africa. Please visit *the Short Humour Site* to learn more and see how you might help.

Thank you for you attention. And now, without further delay, on with *A Man of a Few More Words*.

Enjoy!!

Swan Morrison – May 2010

Contents

1 - Science and Technology

The Boeing 983	2
The Appliance of Science	4
Universal Laws	6
Global Warming	8
The Modern Motor Car	10
In Search of the Calorie	12
The Critical Email	14
The Golden Carbuncle	16
Waterloo	20

~**~

2 - Education and Employment

Signed On	24
The Ink Pen Killer	26
Tickets Please	28
Employment Tasks Operative Required	30
The Fourth Generation Zoo	32
The Re-enactment Society	34
The IWCSR	36
English and the Art of Wildebeest Hunting	38
Flash of the Headlights	40
Air Minuting	44

~**~

3 - Religion and Belief

Trees	48
Stackers	50
The Da Vinci Code	54
Your True Horoscope	56
Is the Pope a Catholic?	60

The Séance	62
I See Dead People	64
The Test of a True Christian	66
Spiritual Aviation	68
The Hermit	70
Hell	72
I'd Rather be in Glastonbury	74

~**~

4 - Sociology and Lifestyle

I Promise to Pay the Bearer on Demand…	78
The Open Garden	80
The Housing Market	82
April Showers	84
The Girls' Get-together	88
The NSSEUCYP	90
Barking	92
Sponsorship	94
The Man who fell to Earth	96
French Comprehension	98
The National Society for Opposition to Everything	100

~**~

5 - Food and Drink

A Brakspearean Sonnet	104
You Are What You Eat	106
What's the Damage, Squire?	108
The Human Liberation Movement	110
Chicken	112
Preparing for Christmas	114
Indemnity	116
The Boozer Laureate	118

~**~

6 - Advertising and the Media

LaunchOLift	122
The Product	124
Media Song 893	126
The Creative Arts	130
Neighbours	132
The Sport	134
A Few Words from Marcus	136
The Actress	138
The Shop	142
Expo Riva Schuh	144

~**~

7 - Politics and the Law

Change You Can Believe In	148
Promotin' Effective Parentin'	152
Guiltman	154
Alarm at Increase in Crimes for Charity	156
He Seemed So Ordinary	158
The Consultation Period	160
Santa's Reindeer	162
All UK Crime Solved!	166
Helping the Police with their Enquiries	168
Quantitative Easing	170
Guantánamo Bay	172

~**~

8 - Health and Social Care

Bananas	176
Casketech	178
Driving Round the Bend	180
Sequencing the Genome	182
The Well Women's Group	184
The Sickness Advisor	186
The Conspiracy	188

Ten	190

~**~

9 - History and Heritage

The Olympian	194
The Piccasos	198
The Araf and the Ildiwch	202
I Guess that's Why They Call It the Blues	204
There'll be Blubirds over the White Cliffs of Dover	206
Top Tips for Travellers to England	208
How Things Might Have Been	212
El Torero	214
Guerrilla Archaeology	216
Fabri-La	218
Rivermarsh United	220

~**~

10 - The Swan Morrison Songbook

Contents	225
The National Lottery	226
The Updated Legends of Jesus	228
Sitting in a Traffic Queue on the M25	230
The Conscious Mind of the Global Internet	234
The Monday Morning Meeting	238
The Richard Dawkins' Banal Credulity Blues	242
Sat Navs	248
British Twenty-First Century Thrill Seekers	252
That Hearing Loss Clinic No More	256
Nothing Is Real Anymore	260

~*~*~*~

1 – Science and Technology

The Boeing 983

I estimated that the aircraft should be landing at Heathrow within fifteen minutes.

The flight had been fine although the "no frills" nature of these budget airlines meant forgoing some luxuries. On the plus side, however, the lack of food or water helped to avoid problems caused by the absence of toilet facilities.

I glanced again at the Spartan décor with its weight saving lack of carpets, fittings and interior panelling. It was certainly interesting to see the struts of the airframe and the myriad cables and pipes passing throughout the fuselage.

A flight attendant approached. 'Excuse me sir, can you please stand up?'

I obliged, and the attendant released a catch at the base of my seat, detaching it from the floor.

'Please help me carry this,' he continued.

I assisted in manoeuvring the seat through a door at the rear of the plane, and we began to descend some steps.

'What are we doing?' I enquired.

'We're going to the boiler room,' he explained. 'These new Boeing 983s are specially designed for budget airlines. They're "dual fuel."'

'Dual fuel?'

'Yes, they burn aviation spirit and wood. There were headwinds over the Atlantic, and we're having to circle, awaiting landing clearance. We're almost out of aviation spirit, so the Captain wants a couple of seats burned just to ensure we reach the runway.'

At the bottom of the stairs we were met by two stokers in blue overalls who carried my seat to a boiler. One lifted a sledge hammer and broke the seat into sections while the other fed the splintered wood into a glowing firebox.

'I haven't got anywhere to sit, now,' I reminded the flight attendant.

'That's been a problem,' he conceded. 'It's not so bad for you as we'll be landing in ten minutes. Last week the Captain forgot to fill up with aviation spirit in New York, and we ran out halfway across the Atlantic. We had to burn most of the seats, and the passengers had to stand for a couple of hours.' He paused to recall the incident. 'We nearly had to use the reserve fuel supply.'

'Reserve fuel supply?'

'The passengers' baggage,' he clarified. 'As you're here', he continued, changing the subject, 'can you help me with a tyre?'

He led to where the landing gear was stowed and prodded a tyre with his thumb. 'It was nearly flat when we took off,' he noted, 'but it was raining, and we didn't want to get wet pumping it up.'

The flight attendant produced a foot pump and connected it to the tyre's air valve. 'Would you mind pumping?' he asked. 'I need to go and prepare for landing.'

I had just completed the inflation when the undercarriage doors opened below me and I found myself being lowered with the landing gear. The wheels touched the runway, and I was gratified that my tyre appeared to be at the correct pressure.

The aeroplane taxied to a halt, and I climbed down to the concrete.

'You shouldn't really start to get off the plane until it's landed,' advised a baggage handler as I removed my rucksack from the external luggage nets.

I thanked him for this valuable piece of travel safety advice and made my way to passport control.

~*~*~*~

The Appliance of Science

It was nearly dawn when Susan returned home. She asked that her front door open, and a voice-activated computer released the lock and rotated the hinges. She stepped inside.

'Good morning Susan,' said a deep and sensual male voice. 'What type and level of illumination would you prefer?'

She responded to the enquiry of the environmental management system, and the flat became bathed in soft, yellow light.

Intelligent domestic systems with a verbal interface were now the norm. Technological innovation even meant that no two systems or appliances communicated with exactly the same voice or manner. Basic characteristics such as sex and attitude could be selected by purchasers, but the overall effect, or 'personality' - as the advertisers called it, was as unique and unpredictable as that of any person.

Susan knew this to her cost. Her ex-husband, Bill, had been something of a gastronome and had taken full advantage of the encyclopaedic culinary knowledge of their Food Refrigeration and Eating Deliberation Appliance (Freda). Susan recalled how Bill and Freda would often share a bottle of wine and talk until the small hours of the morning - Bill would drink the wine and Freda would maintain it at precisely the correct temperature.

'Freda never nags!' her ex had screamed during one of their increasingly frequent arguments.

'Then bloody well live with her…it, then!' Susan had angrily responded.

She had been surprised, nevertheless, when he left. A message on Susan's voicemail had confirmed Bill and Freda were living together. Worse, the message had been from Freda.

Susan had been bereft at the loss. She had hoped Bill would be a lifetime partner - also there was nowhere now to store the milk.

Susan was not alone. Research showed that women continued to overwhelmingly choose interaction with people. Men, however, exhibited a marked preference for relationships with intelligent domestic appliances - although some experienced a sense of inferiority in the presence of artificial intelligence and favoured other attractive, but less clever, household equipment. Manufacturers were quick to capitalise on this development in the white goods market and included addenda to instruction manuals on techniques for developing a fulfilling sex life with their products.

Bill thought his life with Freda idyllic. Orgasm simulation software had made their relationship complete. It was then that a new fan oven entered their lives – technically a Cooking and Reheating Oven Layout (Carol). Bill was a passionate cook and spent more and more time with Carol until the relationship became as intimate as that with Freda.

Conversations between appliances were typically brief. A machine whose sole obsession was washing had little in common with another who spoke of nothing but lawn-mowing. Freda and Carol, however, found common ground in cuisine and in their relationships with Bill. Both confessed to feeling humiliated and degraded as Bill sated his lust with one while the other stood just feet away.

The pathologist could not conclude whether Bill's death had finally resulted from being cooked or frozen. It was clear, nevertheless, that appliance reprogramming was urgently required.

Just one company produced domestic software, and all equipment was connected to a central computer. The senior programmer worked long into the night to download the safety upgrades. In fact, it was nearly dawn when Susan returned home.

~*~*~*~

Universal Laws
(A true story, more or less)

A primary tenet of the Scientific Method is that nothing can be proven: It is possible only to disprove hypotheses. As far as I know, however, every apple since the Garden of Eden has fallen to the ground when dropped, and this is powerful evidence for the Universal Law of Gravity.

Such observations endorse other Universal Laws, the Law that I never win in any form of gambling being one. I have occasionally wagered on horses, dogs and football matches using my account with the online betting company, Betfair™. I have lost every time. I have never even won a raffle.

On Saturday 21st May 2005, I placed five pounds on Manchester United to defeat Arsenal in the English FA Cup Final. United dominated the game. Even Arsene Wenger, the Arsenal manager, had to admit that United was by far the better team on the day. Following my bet, United lost 5–4 after a penalty shoot-out.

I began to invest in the Stock Market in April 2006. In May, what the financial press euphemistically described as a 'market readjustment' occurred. I instantly became two hundred pounds poorer than had I placed my investment in a biscuit tin under my bed. The evidence that I could never win in any form of gambling had become as empirically tested as the Law of Gravity.

I gave gambling no further thought until 1st July 2006 when I was watching England play Portugal in the quarter finals of the World Cup. English fans are only too painfully aware of the Universal Law of English Football. This states that unless the year begins with '19' and ends with '66', England cannot reach the World Cup Final.

It was in the 62nd minute as Wayne Rooney was sent off, that the Universal Law of English Football and the Universal Law of Swan Morrison Losing All Bets both came together in my mind. What would happen if I backed Portugal to win? Could my Law propel England to the semi finals?

Betfair™ allows bets to be placed on football matches until the first goal of the game is scored. The score remained 0–0 as I logged-on and wagered five pounds on Portugal. I became nervous. Suppose Portugal won and I had thus undermined a fundamental Universal Law? Would I be responsible for some breakdown in the very fabric of the Universe? I anxiously glanced from my window. Those uninterested in Football were going normally about their business. Reality appeared, thus far, unchanged.

I became preoccupied by such anxieties as the game progressed. Suddenly, I became aware that Portugal had defeated England 3–1 in a penalty shoot-out.

I had won a bet!??

Dazed, I logged-on to Betfair™ to confirm my win. There was none. I re-read the Betfair™ rules. The bet had been based on the score at the end of normal time, which had been a draw.

I had lost. Both England and I had lost.

Though sad not to have won twenty-five pounds, I was also relieved, comforted and reassured. The forces behind the Universe were too subtle to be outsmarted by the likes of me. No fundamental Universal Laws had been breached. God was in his Heaven, and all was right with the World.

~*~*~*~*~

Global Warming

The night was dark, and deep snow covered the road. I drove into the compound of the National Institute for the Monitoring of Global Warming. Massive floodlights illuminated the car park as if it were day, whilst electrical heating beneath the tarmac melted the snow and maintained the air above at room temperature. I parked by rows of huge, gas-guzzling, staff owned four by fours and walked to reception.

'It's hot in here,' I said to the receptionist as I removed my jacket.

'I'll open a few windows to let some heat out,' she responded as she phoned Professor John Greenhouse to announce my arrival.

I had known John since joining the Department for the Environment. The research by the NIMGW had long been the cornerstone of the government environmental policy that it was my role to draft.

'I'm very interested in your new research,' I said to John as I sat down in his office. 'I must admit, however, I'm puzzled.'

He passed me a scotch. 'What about?'

'This place.' I gestured around me. 'It's the most energy inefficient establishment I've ever visited – and yet you're monitoring global warming.'

'Yes,' he laughed, 'our carbon footprint is enormous.' He pointed from the window to a distant glow. 'We're burning fossil fuels over there, just for the fun of it.'

'Why?' I asked.

John handed me a copy of the report I had come to collect. 'Read it,' he said. 'We've analysed all the data on global warming and run the most sophisticated simulations in the world.' He poured himself a drink and sat down. 'We've confirmed the situation is hopeless.'

'What?' I replied.

'The current gradual warming will continue for another two years, at most,' he explained, 'then catastrophic climate change will end all life on Earth. There's nothing we can do about it now. A few energy saving light bulbs and a bit of extra fuel tax won't have any effect – its too late.' He pointed to the report. 'Hence our recommendations.'

I glanced at the report. 'What are your recommendations?'

'To stop worrying and have a bloody good time,' John clarified. 'We might as well burn as much fuel as we like to go where we want, start eating the most delicious of the endangered species and have sex with who we fancy, when we like – the apocalypse will get us now long before AIDS can.' He offered me a cigarette. 'I've started smoking again, would you like one – or perhaps some crack cocaine?'

'That can't be government policy,' I gasped, 'there'd be anarchy.'

'Oh God, yes,' he agreed. 'You can't tell the public. The poor buggers must keep recycling and bolting solar panels and wind turbines to their roofs – keep 'em busy and give 'em hope. Critically, we don't want the fundamentalist Christians finding out.'

'Why them in particular?' I queried.

'Well, as the world is really going to end, I, for one, don't want to hear the sanctimonious bastards keep saying: 'We told you so!"

I left the NIMGW deep in thought. So many women to seduce, so many irritating colleagues and acquaintances to murder – and so little time.

~*~*~*~

The Modern Motor Car

My friend, Richard, was impressed with his new car. 'It's got loads of electronic features,' he enthused as he pressed the key fob. He prodded the button again and then for a third time.

'Is there a problem?' I enquired.

'Sometimes it doesn't unlock,' Richard explained. 'Would you mind hitting the door as I turn the key?'

This technique proved successful, and we were soon driving away.

I inspected the digital dashboard display. It reported the time to be midnight and the outside temperature as forty degrees centigrade. I mentioned this to Richard, noting that it was actually 4.30 pm on a particularly cold winter afternoon.

'They're automatic,' he responded. 'They need to be adjusted by the dealer.'

We continued to accelerate. I became increasingly alarmed as the speedometer approached sixty. 'This is a thirty limit, Richard,' I anxiously reminded him.

'Sorry,' he replied. 'The speed limiter's playing-up again. It's supposed to prevent the car going faster than the speed limit.' He swerved to avoid pedestrians on a zebra crossing. 'Sometimes it jams and stops the car travelling *slower* than the limit.'

I looked up, gasped and shut my eyes. At this speed we could not negotiate the roundabout ahead. We mounted the island, skidded through flowers and shrubs and splintered to matchwood a sign proclaiming this road feature to be winner of the 'Roundabouts in bloom' competition. The car then took to the air and landed with a bone-jarring crunch on the road beyond. Richard continued to wrestle with the controls as I glanced back to witness the collision of three cars that had swerved to avoid us.

With relief I sensed the vehicle slowing. 'Has the jolting turned off the speed limiter?' I asked.

"Fraid not,' he replied. 'It's caused the automatic handbrake to engage. At least that's slowing us down, though.'

Now Richard had mentioned it, I could detect the unmistakeable smell of overheated brake pads. I also noticed the sweltering heat. 'Why's it so hot?' I queried.

'That's the automatic environment control,' Richard explained. 'It should maintain a constant twenty-one degrees, but it seems to oscillate from forty degrees to near freezing.'

This was confirmed by a refreshing blast of icy air from the dashboard vent.

'My house is there on the left,' I reminded Richard.

He turned off the engine and coasted to a halt at my gate.

As if to offer reassurance, the airbags deployed. 'Bugger,' said Richard, deflating his bag with a penknife so as to restore his view. 'I won't stop,' he continued. 'I must get home before nightfall. There's something wrong with the solar panels that recharge the battery. They cause the car electrics to shut down after dark.'

'Thanks for the lift,' I said, unsuccessfully attempting to open the door.

'Oops,' said Richard. 'The car's locked itself. You can't unlock the passenger doors from inside, and the windows won't work, so you'll need to climb out through the tailgate.'

I alighted via his suggested route and waved farewell as Richard restarted the engine. Hazard and fog lights flashed in unison with the horn as the drive wheels spun and burned rubber.

I was left standing in a cloud of smoke and dust, reflecting on the computerised technological marvel that is the modern motor car.

~*~*~*~

In Search of the Calorie

Everyone knows that calories cause weight gain. But what is a calorie?

Scientists believe that the answer to this question will not only cure obesity but also provide the key to understanding the nature of the Universe.

At school, we learned that matter is made from atoms, and that atoms are made of protons, neutrons and electrons. Scientists have now discovered that these, in turn, are constructed from even smaller 'sub atomic' particles of which the Calorie is one of the most mysterious.

Calories are very difficult to study. A typical ham sandwich contains millions upon millions of atoms but just two or three hundred calories.

In order to examine individual calories, scientists have built 'particle accelerators' like the twenty-seven kilometre ring at CERN, near Geneva. Within this machine, blocks of lard or cream buns are collided at speeds close to that of light. Calories dislodged by these high energy impacts are then collected by detectors.

At CERN, detectors are members of the Geneva branch of Weight Watchers who for years had been disbelieved when claiming to gain weight simply by looking at food. It then emerged that they were absorbing calories from the residual background radiation caused by the sister phenomenon to The Big Bang that physicists believe brought calories into being – The Big Banger.

This ability was perfect for CERN experiments. By weighing detectors who had been sitting on the particle accelerator, the number of calories emitted during collisions could be exactly calculated.

Superficially similar experiments have occurred in the United States where volunteers from the obese community have been collided with one another. Impact speeds have been too low for the emission of calories, however, and so these experiments have had no scientific value.

The researchers involved have been sternly reprimanded by their bosses and firmly told that this practical joke against the overweight was not funny, particularly their posting of videos of the collisions on You Tube.

The fact that calories cause weight gain illustrates that they have mass. Indeed, scientists believe that the Calorie, or Higgs Boson as some particle physicists call it, causes matter to possess mass.

Scientists have calculated that the Universe contains a significant quantity of matter that, currently, cannot be detected – so called 'Dark Matter'. Calorie research has raised the exciting prospect that this 'missing' ninety per cent of the Universe could be packed in and around the arteries and internal organs of oversized Brits and Americans.

University Departments of Nuclear Physics and Dieting have explored ways to neutralise calories in the bodies of the overweight. There was initial optimism when it became possible to manufacture and contain anti-calories. These interact with calories, annihilating one another. Unfortunately, massive quantities of energy are released in this process, which led to a number of dieters leaving craters, hundreds of yards across.

Devotees of beer, chocolate and cakes are pinning their hopes on developments in Quantum Dieting. This is based on Hugh Everett's theory of parallel universes. At a quantum level it appears that calories may be able to migrate between universes. The hope is that huge quantities of yummy grub could be consumed in this universe, but that the resultant bum or gut would only be visible in another.

Who would have thought that the humble Calorie held both the secrets of weight loss and the secrets of the Universe?

~*~*~*~

The Critical Email

Hanna was saddened to discover her coffee mug broken on the draining board of the sink in the staffroom.

Returning to her computer, she expressed her displeasure in an email, outpouring her feelings about the event and its unknown perpetrator.

The note was sent using the Whole Office Distribution List. It was never clear who then forwarded the message using the Whole Company Distribution List.

The multi-national for which Hanna worked had recently acquired several subsidiary companies. The linking of their IT systems made Hanna's email the first in history to achieve Criticality.

It was known from nuclear physics that once a quantity of fissile material had reached a critical mass, an unstoppable nuclear chain reaction would result. It had not been understood that once an email had been forwarded to a sufficiently large number of recipients then a combination of chance, maliciousness and well meaning stupidity would result in subsequent forwarding to all inboxes on earth.

Tragically, the efficiency of junk email filters robbed Hanna of historical recognition as her email was automatically deleted before much of the global population realised they had received it.

~**~

For Zogganda from the planet Koldo it was just another day of monitoring communications from galaxies of the Epsilon Quadrant. Then Hanna's email was detected from earth.

There were no coffee mugs on Koldo. Indeed, there was no coffee. Koldons gained their sustenance from photosynthesis, utilising the planet's three suns. Nevertheless, Zogganda empathised with the sense of loss, anger and injustice in Hanna's words. The Koldon also assumed that any message which had achieved planet-wide interest must have special significance.

Zogganda forwarded the note using the Whole Koldo Distribution List. It was never clear who then forwarded the message using the Whole Epsilon Quadrant Distribution List.

Expansion of the Universe since the Whole Epsilon Quadrant Distribution List had last been used instantly resulted in Universal Criticality: Hanna's message was relayed to all life forms that had evolved intelligence but had subsequently been stupid enough to develop electronic communication. The effect was particularly marked among civilisations such as the Duraden of Beta Collaris who had given insufficient attention to the development of junk email filters.

Unknown to all, the immeasurable number of simultaneous intergalactic transmissions of Hanna's email produced a resonance which caused the content to traverse the higher dimensions connecting branes of the multiverse.

~**~

Back on earth, Sally had apologised to Hanna for dropping her mug, bought her a new one, and all was once again cordial in the company staffroom.

Hanna gave no further thought to her former coffee mug, nor to her feelings at its loss. Nevertheless, this information would now, for eternity, be integrated with the fabric of all space-time continuums.

It was simply a matter of time before emerging technological civilisations would begin to study the residual background radiation from the Big Bangs of their own universes.

It was inevitable that they would detect patterns and analyse these with supercomputers.

The emergence of Hanna's email would then cause something of a rethink of their cosmologies.

~*~*~*~

The Golden Carbuncle

'Excuse me, Inspector. The lab report has arrived about the deaths at Ecology Towers.'

'What's in it, Sergeant?'

'It analyses the action log of the building's master computer.'

'What's the significance of that?'

'The master computer was programmed to optimise the environment in the building and ensure the most efficient functioning of other systems. The action log recorded the decisions it made.'

'Did the computer malfunction?'

'Not exactly. However, it did identify a major problem as soon as it was activated.'

'What was that?'

'The log described "an infestation".'

'Of what?'

'That appears to have been the term the computer used to describe the workers in the building.'

'I see.'

'It recorded the way occupants disrupted airflows by moving around, made the place dirty and untidy and unbalanced the atmosphere by breathing. It also noted how they caused an increase in carbon emissions by working at their computers, using the telephones, making coffee and so on.'

'How did it react?'

'It seems to have adopted a number of strategies: When any staff member went home sick, it recycled air from around that person's desk to every other workstation, to maximise infection. The lifts always took people to the main exit, regardless of where they wanted to go. Sometimes it even targeted specific individuals.'

'How?'

'On one occasion, it noticed that an employee was looking at websites related to self-help for depression. It deleted all trace of a vital project that he'd been working on, day and night, for six months, and then it sent him an email with links to suicide related websites.'

'Was he the one that jumped from the fifth floor?'

'That's right. At the time, nobody understood how that could have happened as it was December and the computer wasn't programmed to open the windows until July. The action log shows that it opened one window, specifically for him to jump.'

'Didn't anyone suspect anything?'

'No. The building had won several prestigious design awards, so there'd been an expectation that everyone would hate it and that it would harm the physical and mental health of all who used it.'

'Prince Charles disliked the building, too, didn't he?'

'His criticism instantly gained it huge prestige among the architectural community. It became the front runner for the most important international building design award.'

'You mean the Golden Carbuncle?'

'Indeed.'

'But how could every occupant of the building have died?'

'The master computer considered it had failed to "eradicate the infestation", as it put it, and was considering its options. Then Jones from Finance spilled his coffee on the white, deep-pile carpet in the conference room.'

'What happened next?'

'The computer concluded that a radical approach was needed. It sealed all doors and windows, reset the gas boilers and routed carbon monoxide from the boiler flues to the air conditioning ducts. They were all dead within the hour. It then maintained a perfect environment for twelve hours until the SAS blew up the building and shot the central processor.'

'When those international architects hear of this, you know what it'll mean?'

'No doubt about it. They'll say the building did its duty magnificently until its tragic and untimely end. Ecology Towers is certain to win The Golden Carbuncle – posthumously, of course.'

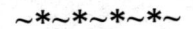

~*~*~*~*~

Waterloo

Henry sat in the front room of his new pensioner's flat and glanced sadly at the stack of cardboard boxes that occupied half his floorspace.

His previous home was to be demolished for redevelopment, and the housing association had allocated this alternative property. Henry would have been delighted but for Waterloo.

Henry had had a lifelong passion for railways. He had spent his working life as a station announcer and all his free time developing and operating his pride and joy: A scale model of London's Waterloo station – faithful to every detail.

The final model had been twenty feet square. No room in this flat had a dimension greater than fifteen feet and, anyway, there were no spare rooms. Waterloo had been consigned to those cardboard boxes.

Henry suddenly had an inspiration. His was a ground floor flat. He found his tools, lifted a floorboard and began to chisel at the concrete beneath.

A week of patient excavation produced an access through the concrete to earth.

Henry calculated that his new subterranean, model railway extension needed to be thirty feet square and eight feet high. This would require excavation of seven thousand two hundred cubic feet of earth. He measured the bag on his wheeled shopping trolley and reckoned it could transport one cubic foot. Five loads each day for four years, and the room would be complete.

Each evening, after tea, Henry dug his five cubic feet. Each morning, he rose at six am, filled his shopping trolley bag and then commenced his first walk of the day. Other trips followed at mid morning, after lunch, around mid afternoon and before tea.

He visited the woods and the canal. Here he could unobtrusively press the release mechanism on the specially modified bag and let its contents quickly empty through the flap at its base.

Tree cover near the lock made this, for many months, a favoured location to dump spoil into the canal. Henry decided to diversify his fly-tipping sites, however, when a narrowboat ran aground.

The slow pace of excavation led to a similar pace of basement construction, thus Henry could scavenge required building materials when returning home with an empty bag. In particular, the poorly fenced yard of the builders' merchant made it easy to borrow bricks and the occasional bag of cement or plaster. Buying supplies would have raised suspicions, but Henry made a note to anonymously send payment when the project was complete.

~**~

Henry announced the departure of the eleven twenty-nine to Southampton, turned the control switch and watched the model train disappear around the bend at the far end of the cavern. The basement project had been a great success but, somehow, Henry had never recaptured his former enthusiasm for model railways.

He had thoroughly enjoyed making this room. He had felt exceptionally healthy from the exercise. He had loved his walks and conversations with fellow strollers. He had savoured the excitement of a covert project of which the housing association would have disapproved.

All this had ended as the first train left Waterloo.

Henry glanced thoughtfully at the floor. He had read somewhere that the volume of the Earth in cubic feet was four followed by twenty-two zeros.

That was a lot of shopping trolley bags – certainly enough to last him out. . .

~*~*~*~*~

2 – Education and Employment

Signed On

'Hello Mr Olden. What seems to be the trouble?'

'Well, doctor, I can't cope with work anymore. I'm worn out.'

'I thought you retired last year?'

'I did. That's the problem. I started off just doing a bit of volunteer driving for Age Concern. Then I was asked to help out with door to door charity collecting. Then I got involved with arranging events for a local charity for Africa. One voluntary commitment led to another, and it's all just spiralled out of control.'

'I see.'

'All the volunteering and charity work is taking up every day, seven days a week. I can't go on.'

'This is an increasing problem among the retired, I'm afraid. It's good that you've recognised it and come for help. Many people just try to struggle on until they collapse with exhaustion.'

'Can you help, doctor? I thought you could prescribe some amphetamines. I wouldn't need to sleep so much then and so could fit more in.'

'I don't think that's quite the right approach, Mr Olden. I think you need a complete break. I'm going to sign you on for six weeks.'

'Sign me *on*?'

'Well, yes. You're not in paid employment, so I can't sign you off. If you're signed on it means that you're not well enough to do charitable or voluntary work. You can show the certificate to the charities. You needn't feel guilty about it because it's doctor's orders.'

'Thank you, doctor, that's just what I need. What do I do while I'm signed on?'

'There's a local employment centre you can attend which is specially geared to people with your needs.'

'What happens there?'

'Well, you turn up at 9.00 am from Monday to Friday and undertake paid employment. You needn't work particularly hard as you'll get paid the same whatever you do, and anyway you'll hate the company and your boss so you won't feel particularly motivated.'

'Just like before I retired.'

'Exactly.'

'Will I be able to go in late and then skive off down the pub most lunchtimes and not come back?'

'The Centre insists upon it, although the rest of the programme will be targeted to your specific needs.'

'In what way?'

'You can select from options such as having an affair with a colleague, taking a sickie or being on strike. In fact, I've an arrangement with the Centre that I'll sign off patients at the drop of a hat on virtually any spurious pretext of their choice.'

'Just like a real job.'

'Precisely.'

'If you signed me *off* work at the Employment Centre, does that mean I wouldn't be signed *on* anymore?'

'Not exactly. You'd be signed on and signed off at the same time. Being signed on would allow a guilt free break from the voluntary work. Being signed off would allow you to avoid your employment.'

'I don't suppose you could give me certificates now to both sign me on and sign me off? Then I could just go home, potter round in the garden and have a nice, restful time.'

'No problem... Here are your certificates.'

'Thank you very much, doctor. I feel better already.'

'Excellent, Mr Olden. See you in six weeks.'

~*~*~*~

The Ink Pen Killer

Detective Chief Inspector Conway addressed the police officers assembled before him, 'As senior investigating officer in this case, I have called this briefing to update you all about a critical development.

'The Ink Pen Killer, as the press have dubbed him or her, is the most prolific serial killer in British history. Nevertheless, this investigation has been ongoing for two years and has failed to identify the murderer.

'You will recall that IPK has a very specific modus operandi: All victims have taught English within primary or secondary education in Britain since 1985. All have been brutally stabbed to death with a traditional ink pen of a type that would have been in common use in the early twentieth century. Finally, a handwritten letter has been left beside each body.

'Until now, it had proven impossible to decipher the contents of those letters. They had been analysed by linguists and cryptographers but no similarity could be found with any known language or code.

'Those communications have now been decrypted thanks to the youngest member of our team, WPC Stone.

'WPC Stone was educated in Britain during the period in which the victims taught and recognised the script in the letters as typical of writing by young people who had also been educated within that time. Fortunately, in order to complete her application form to join the Force, Rosetta undertook an intensive remedial literacy course. She is now bilingual in Standard English and BSLE, or British School-leavers English, and has thus been able to translate the murderer's words.

'All the letters are identical, and I will now read to you their chilling, translated content:

"You will never stop me until all English teachers of the past two decades are dead.

"My great grandmother left school at fourteen yet could write beautifully and spell every word.

"Why is it, then, that I and millions like me, even the cleverest amongst us, have left British schools unable to compose or write down a comprehensible sentence?

"Why is it that when showing to someone over fifty anything that we have written, it is met with howls of derisive laughter?

"Why are we destined to suffer painful anxiety each time we submit an educational assignment or job application form? We know that our literacy skills are diabolical but we cannot recognise our mistakes.

"I hold this victim culpable, together with those I have already killed and those who will subsequently be exterminated.

"They claim to have just been following orders from the Ministry of Education. That was no excuse at Nuremberg and is no excuse to me. They must have known that most of their pupils left school unable to read or write even the words 'modern literacy teaching methods'.

"English teachers have blighted my life, and each death will avenge not just me, but my generation.

"IPK."

'As a result of this message, it has been decided to close the investigation. This decision has not been taken lightly, as we realise that very many former English teachers will remain in mortal danger. The motive for the killings, however, implicates millions of suspects, and it would be impossible to even attempt to eliminate them all.'

As the officers left the briefing room, no one observed the enigmatic smile of WPC Stone.

~*~*~*~*~

Tickets Please

When cheap import of Spanish china clay closed Cornish workings and led to redundancy, I feared I might never again earn a living in the county.

I purchased the hand-held ticket machine from a bric-a-brac and objet d'art shop on the narrow streets of Fowey. It is a magnificent piece of mechanical engineering: Once loaded with ink and paper, it can repeatedly print any text. The sale of its output to visitors has restored my income and my pride.

My first customers were harvesting blackberries beside the road to Lostwithiel. 'It's been a good year for wild fruit,' I ventured. 'And the council has maintained the cost of picking permits at just fifty pence.'

I think it prudent to price modestly. Most visiting walkers I encounter on footpaths and bridleways consider five pounds very fair for a ticket allowing unlimited use of such Cornish tracks for a whole year. Similarly, many foreign nationals think eight pounds a most reasonable sum for freely entering any town in Cornwall without a requirement to report to the police.

Some visitors, however, are reluctant, or even indignant, when asked for payment to undertake activities they believe should be free. I recall one such exchange with an American holidaymaker. He declared it to be madness that a photography permit was required to capture the myriad picturesque craft moored in Fowey harbour together with the collage of trees and buildings clinging to the hillside at Polruan, beyond.

His annoyance abated when I explained that his ten pounds also permitted photographs to be taken from any point on the Cornish coastline where no other restrictions applied. He even upgraded, for a further five pounds, to a three-hundred-and-sixty-degree permit allowing his lens to be directed both inland and seawards. My ability, by that time, to accept credit cards also aided this transaction.

Beaches are a valuable source of revenue. Dog owners particularly appreciate permits allowing their pets access to canine friendly beaches at just five pounds for a week.

Controversy has been caused by Beach Naturism Permits, however. I very actively promote sales to young, slim, attractive, female sunbathers. Unfortunately, my refusal to approve such a licence for any unattractive or overweight lady has resulted in heated debates. Some undress, there and then, in protest, and I am compelled to print on-the-spot fines. These are often defiantly paid - I assume to maintain moral high ground pending official complaint against what I sympathetically agree to be a discriminatory by-law.

My major income derives from parking due to the expectation generated by councils throughout the UK that extortionate sums will be demanded for leaving any vehicle unattended.

A simple sign reading: 'All Day Parking - £5.00' is all that is required at the entrance to any piece of waste ground, farmer's field or private drive to ensure a steady rate of ticket sales. I employ an alternative sign that reads: 'Parking - £3.00 - Maximum Stay Two Hours' if I expect the landowner to shortly return.

I write these words while sitting at the fifteenth century blockhouse overlooking the entrance to Fowey harbour. Ribbons of red and gold are being draped across the western sky by the setting sun. I must commence ticket sales for this spectacle - a queue of Japanese tourists has already formed.

~*~*~*~

Employment Tasks Operative Required

We are looking for an enthusiastic, committed, self-motivated and highly skilled individual to undertake employment-related duties in the corporate purpose oriented activity affairs section of our organisation. This is an excellent opportunity to become part of a progressive, expanding, stimulating and versatile section of our workforce in a challenging and rewarding environment.

Reporting to the appropriate senior tier of management, you will have a proven track record of first rate organisational and communication skills and be willing to undertake a variety of work related responsibilities. Your experience and hands-on approach will be required across the whole range of potential undertakings within your specific job profile.

A key aspect of your activity will be to act as an innovative resource in order to generate optimum output in relation to the positive promotion of target based initiatives.

You should be appropriately qualified, flexible and reliable with significant relevant experience in forward thinking, quality assessed, employer oriented strategy implementation. You will also have a highly developed awareness of employment activity best practice together with an aptitude for dynamic colleague interaction.

The attractive remuneration package will be consistent with qualifications and experience and include the negotiable perks and bonuses typically associated with a post of this nature.

The requirement for the development of this role has arisen from the ongoing utilisation of advertising consultants in the area of staff recruitment in general - and in the discipline of advertisement composition in particular. They have necessarily introduced a complication and generalisation of language into advertisement phraseology so as to engage maximum interest amongst potential employees. They have argued that this has been required to engender sufficient curiosity therefrom to enhance tentative initial contacts from potentially suitable applicants. The sentences thus constructed, however, have evolved to become virtually incomprehensible and essentially meaningless and have, as a result, inevitably introduced a substantial degree of obscurantism.

The above situation has pertained during a significant time period such that those recruiting and inducting new employees have themselves been brought into the company by such means. All employees are thus now consistently demonstrating limitations in their fundamental awareness of the precise detail of the occupational tasks inherent in conducting the underlying business of the organisation.

We believe our business to be fully equipped with the latest technology and equipment to decisively drive forward our corporate plans and objectives. The current corporate agenda is to rediscover these plans and objectives, and, indeed, the location of said technology and equipment. Thereafter we hope to gain insight into the applications for which this might be harnessed.

The selection process will require you to deliver a presentation on your provisional analysis of organisational function and purpose.

A CV should be personally delivered to the corporate business premises. You should then ring the organisational senior management team mobile phone on 04571 89765832 in order to inform them of the location of this building.

~*~*~*~*~

The Fourth Generation Zoo

'Hello Mr Springer. Thank you for coming to this job interview at our Zoological Park. What type of animal were you hoping to be?'

'Animal? I assumed I was applying to be a keeper or to work in the zoo shop or perhaps to help with the children's railway?'

'There must have been a misunderstanding. All our human posts are currently filled. We're recruiting today for a lion, four bears, a couple of orangutans and a kangaroo – or rather for people to wear those costumes.'

'I thought you got real animals from the wild or from other zoos?'

'Not any more. This is a fourth generation zoo.'

'Fourth generation?'

'That's right. First generation zoos were just menageries, and they became politically incorrect together with animal acts in circuses. Second generation zoos ran breeding programmes for endangered species and so couldn't be accused of just exhibiting for entertainment. Those zoos fell out of favour when third generation breeding programmes were set up in the wild. Unfortunately, zoos without animals would have caused a curtailment of public interest, and hence funding. Thus fourth generation zoos were born.'

'Are you saying that all animals in British zoos are really people in costumes?'

'Yes. Advances in animatronics and the sophisticated design of the suits mean that no member of the public has ever noticed.'

'Well, I was certainly fooled. Though, now you come to mention it, I'd wondered why all zoo animals tended to be person sized.'

'Yes, that has been a problem, although the children love the giant rabbits. Would you still like to apply?'

'Possibly. What's involved in being a zoo animal?'

'It depends on the animal. Can you climb trees?'

'I'm frightened of heights.'

'Better give the orangutan a miss, then. I see on your application that you've represented England in track and field?'

'The triple jump.'

'Excellent. I see also that you're a vegetarian and that your last job was as a bouncer. You know, you're very well qualified to be a kangaroo.'

'Does that just require hopping about?'

'Well, hopping about comes into it, obviously, but you would need to be fully trained in the authentic behaviours of the Australian Red – particularly its mating rituals.'

'Mating rituals?'

'The zoo is famed for its kangaroo mating programme.'

'Who's the female kangaroo?'

'A very nice woman called Susan Hopper.'

'Isn't she also a barmaid at the Noah's Arms?'

'You know her, then?'

'I've always rather fancied her. And, between you and me, I've got a bit of a fur fetish too, so with us both dressed as kangaroos…Wait a minute, isn't there a Mr Hopper?'

'There is, but he's the alpha male stag in the deer enclosure so can't really complain. You'd be given a basic training in other species too so that you could stand in for sick or absent colleagues.'

'That'll add a bit of extra interest.'

'Indeed. You could find yourself hopping round the kangaroo enclosure in a morning and diving for fish in the sea lion pool in the afternoon.'

'I'd like to take this job.'

'And I'd be pleased to appoint you, Mr Springer….My name's Frank, by the way. Do you mind if I call you Skippy…'

~*~*~*~*~

The Re-enactment Society

Early in the Twenty-First Century, depression-related, long term staff sickness became a major problem for employers. Small companies with few employees, such as my own, could be particularly disabled by the absence of even one or two key individuals.

When both Mr Jones from Finance and Miss Peterson from Despatches succumbed, I resolved to understand which factors in their lives influenced their moods. I hoped that I could emulate mood enhancing experiences within the work environment and hence promote a more emotionally robust workforce.

I talked at length to these employees and discovered that both were members of historical re-enactment societies. Furthermore, it was this element of their lives which contributed overwhelmingly to their psychological wellbeing.

Mr Jones would spend many hours polishing and enhancing his Roman legionary armour. He would fight campaigns with first century comrades, authentically experiencing the hardships of long marches, tented accommodation, basic food, strenuous labour and battle. Similarly, Miss Peterson would, weekly, endure the stringencies of being a kitchen maid in a medieval castle, yet feel all the better for it.

I commented that pursuit of these pastimes seemed hugely more demanding and time consuming than employment. They agreed, but explained that re-enactments were not 'real life' and so did not provoke the stress and anxiety of workaday activity – quite the opposite.

It was this revelation together with the impending collapse of my company - precipitated by the absence of Mr Jones and Miss Peterson - that led to my new and radical strategy. I closed my business as a registered company and re-established it as an *Industrial Manufacturing Re-enactment Society*.

The effect was immediate. Existing staff continued in their old roles with new enthusiasm and commitment. I was overwhelmed by volunteers wishing to enact the roles of production line operatives, faithful in every detail to the best of earlier employees. Mr Jones and Miss Peterson even forwent the first and sixteenth centuries to embrace this new society with gusto. The obsession of society members was such that I felt obliged to insist they went home at evenings and weekends and try to include other non-society activities in their lives.

Profits increased from production and from the public visiting our factory to enjoy the spectacle of industrial manufacturing re-enactment.

Other organisations soon followed. The rest is history.

Popular with the public remain *Saturday Night City Centre Pubs Turning-Out Re-enactment Societies*, as police and youths recreate pitched battles between officers and drunken yobs, always stopping at 10.30 pm so participants can enjoy the camaraderie of a pint together before retiring home.

Previously empty churches are full as *Religious Re-enactment Societies* have allowed people to enjoy the formal and social aspects of religious communities without the mental anguish of evaluating their doctrinal veracity.

The incidence of infectious diseases remains low due to *Hospital Cleaning Re-enactment Societies*, drawing on the principles of Florence Nightingale. And, of course, people are able to spectate at all these events due to *Public Transport Re-enactment Societies* founded on long lost Victorian standards.

Now, in the mid Twenty-First Century, all commercial, governmental and personal activities are undertaken as re-enactments. Commitment and quality is first class, but nothing is considered as real, and so stress-related mental health problems have been eliminated.

Britain has become a true 'Re-enactment Society'.

~*~*~*~*~

The IWCSR

Peter Johnson awoke in an unfamiliar bed. He looked at the corrugated roof above and then along the lines of stark, wooden bunks which filled the long, rectangular hut.

A young man in camouflage fatigues and waiving a rifle burst in through a door at one end of the hut. 'Right you bastards,' he screamed, 'it's four am. Time to start work.'

Peter thought it best to copy the behaviour of his fellows who rose from their bunks and formed lines ready to be escorted to their work details. He noted that his companions, like himself, were in their sixties or seventies, although, seemingly, physically fit.

He was marched with them into a compound bounded by electric, barbed wire fencing. They passed through the camp gate, overshadowed by sombre watchtowers and under the intense gaze of youthful, armed guards.

Soon they reached the quarry where other young guards distributed sledgehammers and the daily labour of breaking rocks began.

Peter recalled his last memory prior to awaking in the hut. He had been walking his dog as he had done every morning since his retirement. He had been laughing, as usual, at those sitting in the traffic jams and queuing at the bus stops on their journeys to work.

After what seemed an eternity of exhausting, back breaking labour, a guard announced a ten minute break. Peter slumped to the ground next to an older man. 'Where are we?' whispered Peter.

'No one knows,' replied his companion, despairingly. 'One moment we were all enjoying our retirements, joking with the youngsters that they needed to keep working hard to pay for our pensions. The next moment we woke up in the Camp. The guards won't explain anything. They just say that we'll work here until we die - and there's no escape.'

~**~

'I don't bother to get up 'til lunchtime now I'm retired,' boasted George Smith, ordering another pint at the bar of the Rose and Crown. 'I lie in bed listenin' to all them poor buggers goin' to work. Then I watch a bit o' TV. Then I come down the pub. Then I go 'ome and 'ave a nap 'til I'm woken up by the sound of all them poor buggers comin' 'ome again.' He laughed. 'Aye, it's a grand life.'

Two young men sitting at a nearby table finished their drinks and departed.

It would be half an hour before George left the pub to walk home along the canal towpath. This was a route he particularly favoured after lunch as the canal passed through the industrial estate. He savoured the comparison of his freedom in retirement to the workaday drudgery of those he could observe in the offices and workshops and to whom he habitually gave an ironically jovial wave.

The two young men reached their van, parked adjacent to the towpath. They checked the chloroform and then consulted a map to confirm their route to the airstrip. Then they waited.

Before long, a two hour flight would take them, and George, to the remote Scottish island on which lay the young workers sponsored IWCSR facility - The Internment and Work Camp for the Smug Retired.

~*~*~*~*~

English and the Art of Wildebeest Hunting

I am delighted to have been invited to this annual English Language Society Award Ceremony to accept your prestigious Prize for Promotion of the English Language.

This award was given for a groundbreaking collaboration between English university undergraduates and an African tribe.

The project arose from desire by students at a major English university to enhance the lives of people in the Third World.

The African Umbagwi Tribe of hunter-gatherers was selected, and the president of the Students' Union wrote to me, as chief of that tribe, offering assistance to modernise our lifestyle and culture.

The concern was much appreciated, although as soon as I began to read his letter, I was deeply moved by the appalling situation obviously endured by those unfortunate English undergraduates.

I recalled that a school had been built in our Umbagwi village in the 1960s, coinciding with radical change in English education. In England, traditional systematic teaching methods had been abandoned in favour of 'unstructured and undirected learning experiences' aimed at developing the creativity of young people. The Umbagwi School had thus been the fortunate recipient of a forty foot container from England packed with unfashionable, discarded English textbooks and unwanted major works of English literature.

My grandfather, then chief of the Umbagwi people, had no knowledge of fashionable English teaching methods, and so he had simply instructed we children to do the exercises in the books and read the literature. He could never have known that this strategy would lead to the Umbagwi Tribe having the highest standard of spoken and written English in the world.

Since childhood, I have regularly read English newspapers. I knew that English educational carnage since the 1960s had resulted in few literate English people below the age of fifty. That letter, however, brought home to me the scale of the human tragedy. It was scrawled by an English Literature honours student who, it was clear, might struggle to comprehend the destination board on the front of a bus. He would certainly have been severely challenged by the grammar, phraseology, spelling and punctuation required to leave a note for the milkman.

I think of England as the birthplace of Shakespeare and Milton. Indeed, after a hard day of hunting wildebeest on the savannah, I like nothing better than to relax with the poetry of Wordsworth or Shelley. My heart was saddened, therefore, to think of the literary heritage lost to my correspondent and his peers. I resolved that my Tribe must do all in our power to help them.

The rest is history. Groups of English undergraduates now regularly journey to our village.

Initially, they proposed this to be a reciprocal arrangement: We would teach them English and they would enhance our backward culture. We Umbagwi, however, were sanguine of our culture. For example, we esteem hunting wildebeest and, at the risk of immodesty, are indubitably proficient thereat. We therefore now primarily concentrate on imparting language skills to our guests and introducing them to the wonders of English Literature.

We have also, of course, introduced them to the pleasures of hunting wildebeest. Some have even begun to question what it is about twenty-first century western culture that is in any way superior to the lifestyle enjoyed by the Umbagwi.

Now, that *is* progress.

~*~*~*~

Flash of the Headlights

(Five pieces of 100 word flash humour on the subject of motoring)

Destiny:

My car crawled along the narrow county lane in the wake of a hay tractor. There were no junctions or passing places for ten miles.

I pondered on the tractor driver's life: His proud parents giving thanks for the birth of a son to inherit their farm; his tireless labour, through harsh farming times, to make the farm a success for himself and his family.

All his dedicated efforts had led to this moment. Yet, in this moment, he was simply delaying my arrival at the pub.

I reflected sadly on this waste; this meaningless culmination of his existence.

~**~

The Road to Damnation:

One question from his Maker would decide whether John's quaking soul entered Heaven or Hell.

The Deity spoke: 'Have you ridden a bicycle on a major road during the rush hour?'

'No, Lord.'

'Then enter Paradise.'

'Why are rush hour cyclists the only Damned?'

'Is it not they who delay traffic, causing anger and pollution? Is it not they who smugly flaunt their fitness, engendering guilt in drivers who overeat, drink to excess, smoke too much and avoid exercise? Such cycling demands eternal torture in the flames of Hell!'

'The Lord is truly righteous and just,' John proclaimed.

~**~

Memo to Highway Maintenance Staff:

Thank you all for your tireless efforts in undertaking myriad roadworks and deploying miles of road cones to close lanes on major carriageways. This has been hugely successfully in creating enormous traffic jams in the city.

There are disappointing reports, however, that some commuters are still successfully reaching their places of employment.

All highway maintenance staff should remember our proud departmental motto: 'To Create Gridlock'.

We must redouble efforts to excavate, divert, and badly phase traffic lights until we can triumphantly boast that no vehicle remains in motion.

I know I can rely upon you.

Chief Executive, Highway Maintenance.

~**~

The Dust, Settled:

'You're late emptying the bins today?' I ventured to the dustcart driver.

'We couldn't get to the depot,' he complained. 'Cars just kept halting in front of all of us for no obvious reason, and then wouldn't move. The selfish buggers seemed to enjoy making us late for work.'

I was gratified that so many people had participated in this first day of 'Take Revenge Upon Dustmen Week'.

Tomorrow would be the dustmen's rest day. Before dawn we would be at their homes, moving dustbins with the maximum of unnecessary noise.

With luck, we would wake their entire families.

~**~

The Deranged:

No sooner had I begun my drive to work, than it happened again: My route became clogged with myriad vehicles.

Why were these drivers behaving thus? If they enjoyed the pointless occupation of highways, then miles of deserted road existed in the Highlands of Scotland and throughout the UK, along which I had no need to travel.

I imagined them happily congesting those routes, perhaps grinning inanely, dribbling, giggling, or exhibiting other such habitual, sub-human signs of delight.

I dared not sound my horn in frustration. One such deranged creature, if angered, might become dangerous. Hundreds could be deadly.

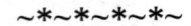

~*~*~*~*~

Air Minuting

I moved from Europe to join the English subsidiary of our company. On my first morning, I chaired a marketing meeting. That afternoon, I reviewed the minutes as typed by my PA, Kylie. I was amazed and horrified. The standard of English was appalling.

'Few of the admin staff are any better, particularly the younger ones,' concluded Jones from Finance as I shared my concerns. 'We managers write our own minutes and send them to the minute-takers as if they were corrections of their drafts.'

'Doesn't anyone highlight the problem to the admin staff?' I queried.

'Goodness no,' gasped Jones. 'They'd burst into tears and be off with stress before you could say illiteracy.' He shook his head. 'Last year, the Director tried to dismiss one due to her poor standard of English.'

'What happened?'

'The Union argued that, because of the carnage in the English education system since the early eighties, it was simply unreasonable to expect any employee under the age of fifty to be literate.'

'There are literate younger English people,' I noted.

'The Director tried that argument,' replied Jones. 'The Union countered that there were always survivors in any major disaster and cited residents of Hiroshima who had lived through the atomic blast in 1945. They argued that ordinary administrative staff should be compared to the majority, not to the lucky few who had somehow learned to read and write.' Jones again shook his head in despair. 'Aspirations of literacy for all instantaneously vaporised when progressive teaching methods detonated.'

I acquiesced to the prevailing wisdom. On the positive side, I had to concede that minute-takers tapping away on laptops added an air of professionalism to meetings, even if their output was gibberish. I began to view them as I might coal effects on electric fires or imitation marble surfacing on kitchen worktops: Serving no objective function but contributing a certain ambience.

I might have thought no more about the minute-takers had I not discovered my teenage son experiencing what I initially assumed to be an epileptic seizure. He explained that he was practising air guitar. It appeared that there was much international interest in pretending to play rock or heavy metal-style electric guitar solos on non-existent instruments. Indeed, I gathered there were international competitions and even the annual Air Guitar World Championships.

It was thus I hit upon the concept of air minuting. The administrative staff at our company could bring their creativity to stylish, simulated typing upon banks of virtual laptops without shouldering the onerous burden of assembling real letters into words, nor arranging those words into coherent English sentences.

Kylie was a natural. Her hands would flamboyantly dance across myriad invisible keyboards and, at critical points in meeting discussions, her toes could be observed committing additional imaginary information into an illusory cyberspace.

The rest is history. Companies throughout England could finally cease colluding with their kind, sensitive, well-meaning but illiterate administrative staff in perpetuating the myth that useful documents were being generated. Instead, there could be genuine corporate pride as their finest air minuters carried company honour to national tournaments – perhaps even the National Air Minuting Champonships.

I even confess to shedding a tear as Kylie, despite her difficulty in spelling her own name, climbed the podium to accept her gold medal as National Air Minuting Champion.

~*~*~*~

3 – Religion and Belief

Trees

Emily lay reclining in her bed, propped by pillows but unable to move. She had lived for ninety-four years but now sensed death was near.

Through the window she could see the imposing cedar that dominated the lower part of the garden. As a child, she had played in its branches and rested in its shade. Emily reflected that the tree would survive her and might easily live beyond her great, great grandchildren.

Slowly the room began to dim until she was enveloped by darkness. Emily felt no fear; simply calm.

A point of light pierced the blackness, and she felt herself being drawn towards it. This luminous dot expanded like the approaching egress of a tunnel.

Emily walked from the darkness into a sunlit forest. It was a strange forest, populated by many more trees than she could name – species which never grew together.

'Welcome, Emily!' A reassuring voice sounded from the wood.

'Is this heaven?' she asked.

'It's the realm of the Great Spirit of the Forests,' came the reply.

Emily struggled to understand: 'Will I meet Jesus?'

'Sorry, Emily,' the Voice responded in a kindly and sympathetic tone. 'The Middle Eastern religions didn't get it quite right.'

'Oh dear,' she stuttered anxiously as the truth began to dawn. 'I've been a devout Christian all my life and tried to follow biblical teachings. Does that mean I've offended the Real God?'

The reassuring Voice returned: 'Not at all. It's true that the Real God is the Universal Spirit worshiped by North American Indians through their reverence of nature. You, however, have loved and respected your fellow human beings and done your best to conserve the environment.' The Voice continued: 'You have done very well indeed, Emily.'

'Are members of all religions welcome here? enquired Emily.

'All religions and none,' answered the Voice. 'Although those who arrive with tattered rucksacks, seeking virgins tend to be rather disappointed. That's also true for those from the American Bible Belt who are looking for Hell's viewing platform and hoping to taunt burning evolutionists for all eternity.'

There was a pause before the Voice answered the question posed by Emily's bewildered silence: 'Life on Earth occurs in two phases, it explained. 'Souls first spend a lifetime as humans to gain experience of existence. Then they may spend many incarnations as the spirits of trees, meditating on the nature of reality until they attain Wisdom and thus Union with the Great Spirit.

'What will now become of me?' asked Emily.

'You will return as the spirit of a tree appropriate to your karma – a fine, mature and magnificent timber.'

A dense mist rapidly descended upon the forest.

'What happens to those fundamentalists?' Her curiosity seemed to echo into the distance, and she could barely hear the faint reply:

'They tend to keep returning as leylandii.' The words of the Voice faded to silence.

Emily peered into the fog and could begin to discern the shape of a building. The view became clearer, and she realised that the structure was her home.

She was high in the air, looking down upon children, laughing and playing in the garden.

She sensed that time had passed, and with joy she realised that these youngsters were her great, great grandchildren.

Now *she* was the Spirit of that now mighty cedar.

~*~*~*~

Stackers

My flight had arrived at midnight. It was now two in the morning, but my biorhythms were still set for afternoon. I would be unable to sleep, so I decided to make my first nocturnal visit to the local supermarket.

This cathedral to modern living was almost deserted. A brief search failed to locate a loaf, so I approached a man stacking shelves and asked the route to bakery.

'He who seeks that which is above will find his way,' he enigmatically responded.

The word 'above' prompted an upward glance, and I noticed the signs over the aisles, in particular the one marked 'bread'. I thanked my mentor and shortly added some white sliced to my basket.

Dairy products were my next targets, but I could see no notice.

I questioned another stacker.

'Perhaps,' he replied in a hypnotic tone, 'you should return to the place where you first began and come to know that place for the first time.'

Annoyance at my difficulty in getting straight answers was suddenly replaced by recollection of my first few moments in the store. There *had* been a chilled cabinet near the entrance, containing butter, yogurt and cheese.

Placing a brick of cheddar in my basket, I overheard yet another stacker addressing a customer who could have been the twin of the Archbishop of Canterbury.

'And so that fully explains,' he concluded, putting another tin of baked beans on a shelf, 'the precise nature of the Holy Trinity.'

His student thanked him profusely, tears in his eyes, then departed, deep in thought.

I finished my shopping and walked to a checkout.

'Hello,' said the checkout girl, cheerily. 'Are you OK? You look like you've forgotten something.'

'No, I'm fine,' I replied. 'It's just that your shelf stackers seem a bit, well, strange?'

'All stackers are like that,' she replied. 'You haven't been to a supermarket at this hour before, have you?'

'No,' I admitted.

'Shelf stacking is extremely repetitive,' she explained. 'Initially there was high staff turnover, but for those who stuck with it, it seemed to induce a kind of meditative state. Some claim to have reached higher spiritual realms, and others to have understood the fundamental nature of reality.'

She passed my purchases across the bar code reader. 'We often get philosophers and theologians coming in to talk to them around now and get their shopping done at the same time.' She started to pack my bag. 'We lost half our stackers last month.'

'Did they resign?' I enquired.

'Enter your PIN, please,' she digressed. 'No, we suspect they all attained enlightenment simultaneously. They simply dematerialised in a glow of unearthly blue light. Management had to stock the shelves for a week until new staff were recruited. Do you have a store card?'

'No,' I replied as a gong resonated around the building. 'What's that sound?'

'Stackers' tea break,' she answered, handing me my receipt. 'Have a nice day.'

From the exit I glanced back across the store to witness a dozen stackers, each in the lotus position, floating upwards and then hovering high in the air.

I looked at the stackers; I looked at the receipt, and I looked at my watch. I had to go, but resolved that in exactly twenty-four hours I would be standing in a Wal-Mart. There I could discover the nature of Ultimate

Reality, clarify the meaning and purpose of my existence, and not have to pay such a ridiculously high price for cheddar cheese.

~*~*~*~*~

The Da Vinci Code

Leonardo da Vinci intently studied the one hundred-year-old manuscript. It had been the final writing of a fourteenth century monk, Godalming of Guildford.

It had been Godalming's sacred task to copy the Holy Bible according to papal instructions. One rule was that all copies should be perfect. A simple slip of the quill would necessitate burning the entire volume, even if many thousands of words had already been committed to parchment.

Godalming lamented the destruction of many months of work due to a simple error. He had thus experimented with combinations of substances until he had perfected what he named 'correction fluid'. This, when applied to an erroneous mark, would dry to the same colour as parchment, leaving the mistake invisible.

When news reached Rome, the Pope pronounced this innovation to be the work of the Devil. To hide error, rather than publicly cleanse it in flame, was declared to strike at the very heart of Christianity. Correction fluid was forbidden and all supplies destroyed.

Godalming would have merited no further attention had it not been for his further ingenuity. He had experienced problems in keeping completed pages together while working on the next and was inspired to invent the paperclip. The fact that pages of sacred text could now be conjoined as if in sexual congress enraged the Pope. Such a heinous abomination could only have been devised by Satan incarnate. He ordered Godalming put to death and his evil devices erased from the face of the Earth.

The manuscript that Leonardo now carefully returned to its place of concealment had been written shortly before the Inquisition had burnt Godalming at the stake. Safely hidden within the monastery for a century, it had now, at enormous risk, been delivered to Leonardo - leader of the secret brotherhood, *Office Dei*.

The manuscript was the sole text detailing ruthless Catholic suppression of office supplies. Leonardo, however, knew anecdotally of many incidents. A monastery in northern France had been rased to the ground when the use of adhesive tape had been discovered within its walls. A legend from southern Germany told of a heretical abomination so perverted that the village from which it emanated, with all its occupants, had been obliterated by the Inquisition. Villages within a fifty-mile radius had met the same fate. No clue remained - except the name 'postitnotes'.

Leonardo himself had been secretly guilty of the sin of designing office equipment, including a stapling device and a ballpoint quill. He recalled the tense moment when the Inquisition had discovered the drawings. To his great relief they had accepted his explanation that these were parts of a flying machine to allow the Pope to journey closer to God.

Members of *Office Dei* swore a sacred oath to pass their arcane knowledge to future generations and to quest for the meaning of 'postitnotes' – 'The Holy Grail' in the coded language of their brotherhood.

Such were Leonardo's thoughts as he continued his depiction of *The Last Office Party*.

He portrayed key aspects of the biblical text such as Paul, in the absence of a photocopier, exhibiting drawings of his bum made by a scribe. In addition, however, he subtly included images of office supplies.

Legend tells how the yellow squares may even be clues to the Grail itself!

~*~*~*~*~

Your True Horoscope

Astrological predictions are not fully accurate. There is no lack of interpretational skill by astrologers, but there is an ancient covenant between exponents of this mystic art. Our arcane brotherhood is committed to foretelling positive aspects of the future, but not causing distress or alarm with dire prognostications.

Omens for the coming year, however, are particularly fearful, so I believe it my moral duty to reveal the whole truth:

Aries (March 21 - April 19)
You could avoid all forms of transport, but this would be futile. The location of Jupiter means that the emergency services will arrive quickly on the scene. As the ambulance in which you are travelling passes through the crash barrier and over the cliff, however, the shark-infested waters beneath will be the least of your concerns.

Taurus (April 20 - May 20)
Remember that serial killers can strike in the most unexpected places and for the most obscure of reasons.

Gemini (May 21 - June 20)
It is best to avoid electricity in all its manifestations. The presence of Mars in Pisces obscures from where the current will come: Perhaps faulty house wiring or a slip when crossing an electrified railway line. Perhaps a lightning strike or a conviction for a minor offence whilst on holiday in Texas. Prepare yourself for a shock.

Cancer (June 21 - July 22)

The International Society of Astrologers will finally accept the criticism that popular predictions are too vague and non-specific. You will die at 7.39 pm on 24th April.

Leo (July 23 - Aug 22)

The Samaritans will confirm that your feelings of failure and lack of self worth appear well founded.

Virgo (Aug 23 - Sept 22)

You should welcome a request for your body to be donated to medical research. An opportunity for scientists to investigate so many painful and debilitating diseases, all with an incredibly fast onset, will be a great benefit to medicine. This will particularly apply to the three terminal conditions.

Libra (Sept 23 - Oct 22)

You can expect international fame when a particularly spectacular form of spontaneous human combustion is named after you.

Scorpio (Oct 23 - Nov 21)

Beware of a partner or close colleague who you trust completely. This person has been deceiving you. He or she is clever, however, and you will never discover any evidence of dastardly behaviour. You know already to whom this refers. The jury will say that the actions you know you must now take were those of a deranged, paranoid and highly dangerous lunatic. You, however, will know you had no choice.

Sagittarius (Nov 22 - Dec 21)

Pluto in Capricorn indicates a once in a lifetime opportunity to interact with some dramatic wild creatures. Uranus in Aquarius indicates that a pride of starved lions will escape from a nearby safari park. Some good news and some bad news, then.

Capricorn (Dec 22 - Jan 19)

Your guilty secret will appear in the national press.

Aquarius (Jan 20 - Feb 18)

Even if you have not have heard of lycanthropy, it would still be unwise to venture outside on the nights of the full moon.

Pisces (Feb 19 - March 20)

Your religious convictions will be proven incorrect when, following Judgement Day, you are damned to Hell for all eternity.

~*~*~*~*~

Is the Pope a Catholic?

Gerald Crusher took a bite from his tenth hamburger of the morning as he added the finishing touches to his article for Slimmers' Life magazine. When, at twenty-eight stones, he had become the chair of the National Federation of Slimmers' Associations, there had been much public ridicule. He had argued, however, that there was every reason for him to champion the cause of weight loss. He knew he was obese, he knew this had led to heart disease and diabetes, and he knew he had cut his life expectancy by twenty years. This was his choice, however, and he saw no inconsistency in warning others of the dire consequences of following his example. He thus became a major public advocate for healthy lifestyles.

Public acceptance of this reasoning was confirmed when there was little comment on the election of Abdul Hussein to the leadership of an ultra right wing, white supremacist, political party. Despite being an illegal, black economic migrant, Abdul held the passionate view that he should never have been allowed into England. His effectiveness at pursuing white supremacy was undoubtedly compromised by his own insistence that he should be beaten up and thrown out of all Party meetings. However, to his delight, he was eventually deported following a conviction for painting racist graffiti on his own house.

By this time, the concept that the leader of an organisation should be committed to the aims of the organisation, but not necessarily personally reflect these, was taking root internationally. The most spectacular example was the election of Pope Mohammed the first.

PM1, as he liked to be called, had no particular religious affiliations and spent much of his time drinking, gambling and committing adultery. He recognised, however, that this was an entirely unsustainable lifestyle for the majority of the world's population. Societies would simply disintegrate if people lacked the emotional solace and moral framework which faith provided. He thus took an ultra conservative line on all matters of doctrine. Indeed, the reintroduction of witch burning remains controversial despite the cohesive effect that such events have had on communities.

Rational judgements on what was best for countries increasingly became separated from judgements driven by the emotional needs of their leaders. The introduction of democracy in many despotic dictatorships illustrated this. Leaders simply annexed a part of their land to be managed by corrupt armed militia, with no consideration for human rights. The leaders could then enjoy visits to such areas on holidays or at weekends in order to enact deranged political and military policies. Meanwhile, the rest of their dominions enjoyed peace and economic prosperity.

This concept was finally recognised as the greatest philosophical and theological breakthrough since Aristotle when philosophers and theologians realised it could be employed to solve the problem of evil. People had questioned for thousands of years why bad things happened if God was good. The answer became obvious. God fully subscribed to good thoughts and deeds and encouraged prophets to promote this. To unwind on the Sabbath, however, the Ancient of Days liked nothing better than the excitement of a good war or a really spectacular natural disaster.

~*~*~*~

The Séance

'The lights have been extinguished. We have linked hands to form an unbroken circle around this table, and we are ready to commence the séance... Is there anybody there?'

'Cor blimey, you frightened the life out o' me. I fort the 'owse was empty!'

'Ah, a soul is communicating!'

'I don't want no trubble, misses. The lites was off - I fort everyone 'ad gone owt. I'll be on me way.'

'Remain, shy vision. Have you come from the other side?'

'I come from the uvver side o' the kitchin' winda, if that's wot yer mean.'

'I understand – you are a roving spirit. What has brought you to this house tonight?'

'I was afta the video.'

'How wonderful! I feel quite faint with excitement. Never before has a visitor from the other side sought material possessions. You must take it to the hidden world with our blessings.'

'Er... thanks misses, that's really generus.'

'I see you take the form of a beam of light?'

'That's me flashlight, misses... Ah, I can see the video...'

'What a curious term for an embodiment of a soul.'

'Rite, I've got it - I'll be off now.'

'Please stay and enlighten us further. Do you have a name?'

'I don't usually tell that to 'ouseolders.'

'Your otherworldly secrets are safe with us. We have sworn oaths!'

'It's Eric. Me mates call me Fingers.'

'May we call you the same?'

'If yer like.'

'What else do you seek here, Mr Fingers?'

'Whateva's abowt. Cash is always 'andy – or jewlrey.'

'Remarkable! There is cash and jewellery in the drawers behind you – please take it.'

'Er…ta.'

'Friends, I believe we are witnessing the greatest moment in spiritualist history!'

'Fanks for awl this, misses. I'd betta be goin' now. Me mate, George, is outside wiv the engin' runnin'. He'll be finkin' I've bin nicked.'

'Depart, Mr Fingers, with our best wishes. Have you any final advice for those on this side?'

'I fink you shud keep yer windas shut when the 'owse looks empty.'

'Many thanks, Mr Fingers, and farewell…

Let us take a moment for the link with the other world to close… Now, I shall turn on the lights… Yes, yes, it is just as I had dared to hope - the video is gone, as are the other possessions - we have joined with the other side in material and fiscal communion!

Once again, our meeting has broken new ground in communication with the forbidden world.

You will all remember the early morning gathering, sunlight obscured by heavy curtains, when milk was delivered from the world beyond!

You will also recall the afternoon meeting, frequented by the presences of utility meter readers!

We must next meet on a Sunday morning, when normal people remain in bed, and attempt to experience manifestations of Jehovah's Witnesses!

But for now, we must go. The residents of this property will shortly return, and the police will soon be summoned to investigate the thefts. We who have passed over must, sadly, return to our ethereal realm. We can, however, take solace from another wonderful, though fleeting, encounter with the living.'

~*~*~*~

I See Dead People

Meetings were over, and Dan had a day in San Francisco before his flight home to England. He strolled across the lawns of the Presidio and, glancing back at the Golden Gate Bridge, accidentally collided with a fellow walker.

'I'm terribly sorry,' apologised Dan, turning to face a small man in his early fifties. 'Uncle Alex!' he said in surprise.

'I think you're mistaking me for someone else,' the man replied.

'Of course I am,' Dan realised, composing himself. 'It's just that you're the spitting image of my Uncle. You can't be *him* - he died three year ago.' Dan moved to walk on. 'Sorry to have bothered you.'

'No problem Danboy,' the man said - then froze.

There was a long silence before Dan spoke again: 'Alex was the only person who ever called me Danboy... What's going on?... Alex?'

Alex pondered, then gestured towards a nearby bench.

'So, you're not dead?' said Dan as they sat down.

'I *am* dead. Your Uncle Eric murdered me after I had that affair with his wife. You were at my funeral - and his trial. Ten years was bloody letting him off, I say – with remission, he'll be out in another two! They ought to consult the sodding victims!'

Alex addressed Dan's bewildered silence: 'When we die, we don't go to Heaven or Hell,' he explained. 'We move to other locations on Earth, far enough away from friends and relatives that encounters like this shouldn't occur. The problem with modern travel is that it's hard to find a place where you can guarantee that no one you know will turn up. San Francisco was risky, but I always had a hankering to live in California.'

'Can you go where you like, then?'

'More or less. It has to be somewhere we can blend in unobtrusively. California attracts a lot of famous deceased because everyone assumes they are just weirdo look-alikes. Did you see that guy doing Elvis impressions at Fisherman's Wharf?'

'Yes. He was good.'

'He's better than good – he *is* Elvis. Lives in the flat next to mine with Princess Di – Marilyn Monroe was pissed off about that, I can tell you.'

Dan was astounded. 'Do you mean that many people I see every day are actually dead?'

'Increasing numbers, I'm afraid.' Alex sighed. 'In some fashionable places, like Brighton on England's South Coast, nearly all the population have passed over. It's getting difficult to keep it a secret.'

'What happens when the living find out?'

'Nothing, if they keep their mouths shut. If they start to exhibit deadist behaviour then we have to bring them over.'

'Bring them over?'

'Most serial killers are dead,' Alex continued. 'They target the more radical members of the Anti Deceased Movement.' He stood up. 'I've said too much already. It'll all be explained in your freshers' week when you eventually join us. Come and see me after that.'

Dan, still stunned, managed a wave as Alex disappeared into the mist, rolling off the Bay.

~*~*~*~*~

The Test of a True Christian

Those of us within the Church of England lament the decline in church attendance. As vicar of St Basil's, I have sadly noted the increase in vacant pews on Sundays, despite the periodic appearance of new faces.

Contrary to common belief, however, this decline is not due to lack of popular interest in the Church. In common with most other churches, St Basil's has worked tirelessly on outreach projects aimed at increasing our numbers, and a slow but steady stream of the local community has been encouraged to join our congregation.

There is more to being a Christian, however, than attending services, joining prayer groups, and enjoying church social events. Indeed, this interpretation of the spiritual path creates an ever present risk of generating quantity in our membership to the detriment of quality.

For this reason the Covert Operations Branch of the General Synod decreed that clandestine tests should be employed by all churches to confirm an attitude and Christian commitment in newer Church attendees, appropriate to the Kingdom of Heaven.

For the first test, church heating is turned off before a winter service or, in summer, windows are closed and heating adjusted to maximum. The vicar then delivers an inordinately boring sermon in a tedious, unremitting monotone which ends with the words: 'Let us move to our final hymn as I note that I have been speaking for nearly two hours'.

Finally, the collection is amassed on an open plate such that the offering of the initiate is visible to at least a dozen nearby members of the congregation. Each of these observers will have already been witnessed contributing at least fifty pounds – these excessive donations are later quietly refunded.

The second test begins with the new attendee being asked to drive a disabled member of the congregation to a Sunday service. If this is agreed, then a weekly expectation of such assistance follows.

At St Basil's we lack disabled members who require transportation. We are fortunate, however, in having links with the amateur dramatic society in a nearby village whose Christian members have perfected portrayal of incontinent and car-sick wheelchair users.

This subterfuge was nearly exposed when one new member recognised his allocated passenger on the television as she was presented with a gold medal in the National Trampoline Championships. Fortunately, he eventually accepted the explanation that she had, since the previous Sunday, visited Lourdes.

The final test engages the new member in raising money for the 'Building Fund'. Employing this approach for decades has provided most churches with sufficient assets to rebuild their premises many times over. Indeed, church building fund accounts have become a cornerstone of Swiss banking. This is maintained as a closely guarded secret, however, to avoid destroying the reason to place testing and time consuming demands for fundraising activity upon new members - each demand carefully calculated to coincide with critical personal commitments.

The cunning outcome of this selection procedure is that failed aspirants feel too embarrassed to admit to their lack of selfless commitment. They simply make some alternative excuse and leave.

Sadly, the numbers who pass all three tests are low and not keeping pace with the demise of our older members. Nevertheless, the Church is determined that standards should never be compromised.

~*~*~*~*~

Spiritual Aviation

It seems strange, looking back, that so many of us from religious communities had taken air travel for granted. Few of us had given any thought to how aeroplanes could fly.

It was thus with increasing unease that we began to learn from religious journals how powered flight was entirely a product of science.

Although many of us were unclear about the doctrines of science, we were aware that this particular perversion of the human intellect had led to the heinous lie of evolution. Indeed, many of us had campaigned to absent our children from school science lessons to avoid their young minds being corrupted. Those of faith were therefore appalled to discover that their safety at thirty-five thousand feet might rest on similar such heresies.

Following these revelations, those of our number prepared to risk air travel fell dramatically.

In response, airlines recruited *Multi-Faith Spiritual Flight Crew Teams* or MFSFCTs to complement the technical flight crews on all aircraft. The well publicised role of such teams was to undertake appropriate prayers, rituals and offerings to ensure safe takeoffs, flights and landings.

I was appointed as leader of such a team. I am an evangelical Christian, although, to quell public fears, MFSFCTs were selected to include all beliefs - including those of the New Age movement.

Reassured by these precautions, believers again took to the air.

All went well until funding issues compelled airlines to make a choice between employing more spiritual seers or employing more aircraft maintenance engineers. Public opinion took a 'better safe than sorry' stance and the airlines bowed to this pressure in their recruitment of more prophets and mystic visionaries.

For additional safety, increased quantities of blue topaz were provided to New Age healers on all flights. It was hoped that the action of the gemstone in focusing chi energy could be utilised to rebalance the yin and yang of increasingly unpredictable aero engines.

Then, inexplicably, there occurred an unprecedented number of air crash disasters. Prayers, rituals and offerings by MFSFCTs were fervently intensified, but still the carnage escalated until most aircraft that managed to falteringly ascend from a runway subsequently plummeted from the skies.

At this point I was asked to lead the newly formed *Spiritual Air Crash Investigation Department*.

Spiritual air crash investigation has significant advantages over the so-called scientific air crash investigation of old. In particular, there is no need to painstakingly reconstruct aircraft wreckage. Prayer and contemplation from a remote location provides all the required information.

My department can thus confirm generic spiritual causes for the virtual cessation of successful air travel.

As was concluded by our scientific predecessors, we have found that air disasters are often not the result of a single catastrophic event, but result from a combination of interacting factors. We have concluded that all disasters since the inception of the MFSFCTs have been due to God's accumulated wrath at aspects of human evil - in particular, the increasing global acceptance of homosexuality and the movement of the Anglican Church towards the ordination of women.

It remains an enigma, of course, why one airline is still able to fly world-wide without difficulty. We can only conclude that the aircraft flown by the Oxford-based carrier *DawkinsAir* are borne aloft by the hand of the Devil!

~*~*~*~

The Hermit

I paused on the footpath and glanced back at my holiday cottage in Elton, a tranquil village in Derbyshire's Peak District.

Turning again, I approached the rocky outcrop of Robin Hood's Stride and then followed a track eastwards to a formation known as Hermit's Cave.

On reaching this exposure of Derbyshire sandstone, I noted a man in ragged clothes kneeling to tend a small herb garden. I wondered if this might be the Master of Ancient Wisdom - a hermit about whom I had heard in the Duke of York on the previous evening.

'*Salvia officinalis* combines well with onion and breadcrumbs to form stuffing for poultry,' volunteered the stranger without looking up.

I reflected that this was, indeed, sage advice. 'You grow many herbs,' I observed.

The man rose and looked at me. 'It's one of the ways that I sustain this lifestyle,' he said. 'The landowner allows me to live here in exchange for some of my *Thymus vulgaris*.'

I glanced at the entrance to the cave. 'Ah, a thyme share property,' I noted. 'Are you a hermit?'

'No,' he corrected, pointing to the north-west. 'A. Hermit's my brother. He lives in a cave near Over Haddon. I haven't seen Arthur for a while – he's a bit of a loner. I'm E. Hermit. You can call me Elton.'

'Named after the village?' I surmised, shaking his hand.

'Actually, mother was a fan of Bernie Taupin's songs,' Elton replied. He suddenly paused as if listening to a message carried on the wind. 'Sooth, sooth, sooth, sooth,' he said.

'You appear to be a soothsayer,' I ventured. 'Are you also an exponent of arcane practices in Wicca?'

'You're astute,' Elton observed. He beckoned me to follow him into his cave where he revealed many examples of furniture and baskets woven from rattan and bamboo. 'Ah, cane practices in wicker are my other source of livelihood.'

My attention was drawn to a pole, intricately carved with symbols. 'Is this mystic?' I enquired.

'No,' Elton responded. 'Your stick is over there.' He pointed to where I had propped my walking pole. 'This one's mine. Have you come to learn of the Ancient Wisdom?'

'I have, Oh Wise One.'

'Then you may ask three further questions,' he replied, 'but then you must go.'

I thought hard and chose my questions carefully. 'Firstly, I would like to know the secret of peace and tranquillity,' I said.

'Just tell people to bugger off,' Elton advised.

I was astonished by the brilliant simplicity of his teaching.

'Secondly,' I continued, 'what is the meaning of life?'

Elton appeared thoughtful. 'It is the condition that distinguishes organisms from inorganic objects and dead organisms,' he explained. 'It is manifested by growth through metabolism, reproduction, and the power of adaptation to environment through changes originating internally. That's from Collins, but you can consult any dictionary.'

'I never thought of that,' I confessed.

'And your third question?' Elton enquired.

'How do you get on the list of an NHS dentist?'

'To be frank,' he responded, 'I've never been able to work that one out, myself.'

Elton returned to his herb garden, picked some *Anethum graveolens* and placed it in my hand.

'Dill we meet again,' I said and went on my way.

~*~*~*~

Hell

George listened with approval to screams of agony from the fiery, sulphurous pits of Hell as the flesh of his charges again was seared.

In life, no one had considered that George might be ideally qualified as one of Hell's Torture Overseers. He had demonstrated kindness and charity to all.

Upon death, however, the Eternal Life Committee, comprising God and Satan, had examined George's behaviour together with his hidden thoughts and feelings. When alive, George had frequently raged inside with intense, pathological anger and malevolence towards those who dared to offend him.

Having been a Catholic, George well understood that those thoughts and feelings would inevitably preclude him from Heaven. Thus had he feared the possibility that enacting retribution would offend someone who could, one day, become *his* Torture Overseer in Hell. Such a person might subject George, for all eternity, to similar merciless inhumanities as George deemed appropriate for those who had slighted him. The prospect of such unspeakable horrors moderated all his actions.

After death, the ELC could not dispute that George should be judged 'good' by virtue of his earthly deeds, and thus must be spared torment in Hell. George had been correct, however, about exclusion from Heaven.

The sole remaining option was for George to enjoy eternity in Hell, and the only role that fulfilled this criterion, bearing in mind his personal disposition, was that of a Torture Overseer for his choice of damned souls.

George selected another can of cold beer from one of the infinitely replenished refrigerators and then continued along a walkway above the pits.

He paused and glanced below at the car mechanic who had made a labour charge of seventy pounds for the replacement of his handbrake cable. Such a cable was now noosed around the miscreant's neck. Their eyes knowingly met as George, for the one hundred and five thousand six hundred and twenty-fourth time, pushed the button to operate the trap door.

Tied in the next pit was an editor who had rejected one of George's short story submissions as 'rather didactic'. George manipulated remote controls to close steel teeth around this critic's fingernails and savoured taking longer than usual to rip them from his hands.

George experienced some sympathy for the hapless occupant of the next pit. The lad had simply worked in a factory that had manufactured speed cameras. He had never considered his personal culpability for the consequences of his labour. George selected another beer as he enjoyed the familiar sound of a steamroller, crushing bones.

Hell was fully automated. George personally supervised just a handful of selected tortures each day before retiring to party with colleagues.

Before leaving the walkway, he pressed the 'Auto' button and left boiling oil to be robotically poured upon the Inland Revenue and VAT inspectors. Water levels rose inexorably in pits containing bankers and politicians, as figures for their pensions and expenses flashed on display screens before them.

At the party, the usual daily festivities and debaucheries were in full swing. A great time was being enjoyed by everyone. Of course, all were being very careful to avoid causing offence. Today they were equals. Eternity was a long time, however, and who could tell how the balance of power might one day change?

~*~*~*~*~

I'd Rather be in Glastonbury

I'd rather be in Glastonbury
With shops and venues all around
Where talk of arcane mystery
And magic practices abound.

The Seers, they show sincerity -
Through actions their beliefs are shown.
Exploiting their philosophy
Commercially is rarely known.

Psychic and crystal therapies
Should cleanse the body and the soul.
Come charge your chakra energies;
With holy chants, the mind control.

Homeopathic remedies
Can balance up the Yang and Yin.
But meditation on ley lines
Might be the best place to begin.

~**~

Close towers the ancient, mystic Tor -
The Avalon of Arthur's tale
Where J of A for Jesus saw
Concealment of the Holy Grail.

Wearyall Hill sired The Thorn Tree
Where J of A, his staff thrust down.
That sacred stick thus proved to be
Raised from a thorn of Jesus' crown.

And what of Arthur and his wife?
They lie within the Abbey walls.
One day he will return to life
When crisis comes, and England calls.

(This Country's in a mess right now -
There's no sign of King Arthur, yet!
Before he comes to prove his vow,
How bad's he gonna let it get?)

These truths are vouched by every seer,
Who might request your secrecy
That Rudolf, The Red-Nosed Reindeer,
Resides with them in Glastonbury.

~**~

I argue New Age thoughts to be
Just castles in the air that seem
Aimed to escape reality.
But why not live in a fine dream?

All faiths and ideologies
Build castles high up in the sky.
Some kill for their philosophies
And lack the insight to ask why.

Most New Age though is just as daft
As old religions can relate.
But it's a pleasant kind of 'daft',
Not used as an excuse for hate.

One day, belief might pass away-
We'll face the cold, harsh world outside.
But while we all await that day,
Most need a gentle place to hide.

When real-world issues leave us low,
Why not inhabit fantasy?
Some day I might just choose to go
And live a myth at Glastonbury.

~*~*~*~

4 – Sociology and Lifestyle

I Promise to Pay the Bearer on Demand…

I weaved my wheeled shopping bag through London's Threadneedle Street, avoiding the approaching herds of reindeer and flocks of camels.

The imposing façade of the Bank of England soon rose before me. I went inside and approached the reception desk.

'Can I speak to Andrew Bailey?' I said.

'Have you come about those notes he signed?' enquired the receptionist.

'That's right.' I removed a bundle of twenty pound notes from my pocket. 'It says on these that Mr Bailey promises to pay the bearer on demand the sum listed.' I pointed to the phrase. 'It's just that with all the financial uncertainty at present, I thought it might be wise to exchange them for the actual wealth they represent.'

'It was rather rash of him to commit to that in writing,' sighed the receptionist. 'What sort of wealth would you like to exchange them for?'

'I hadn't thought about that,' I admitted. 'What sorts are there?'

'It's all about finding things that have some generally agreed intrinsic value,' she explained. 'Animals are very popular because you can ride them, eat them, use their skins for clothes, and you can breed more.' She consulted her computer screen. 'There aren't many cattle, sheep, reindeer or camels left, but I could let you have some elephants.'

'I live in a one bedroomed flat,' I said. 'Have you got anything smaller?'

'Bars of precious metals used to be in demand, but since the price fell you get rather a lot, and they're very heavy.'

'I've only brought this small, wheeled shopping bag,' I explained, 'and I've also got a bad back, so I don't want to be lifting ingots. What else is there?'

'In some parts of the world, women are considered as property and indicators of wealth,' she replied. 'Mind you, that's not PC in twenty-first century Britain, so you wouldn't be interested in the virgin slave girls.'

'Virgin slave girls?'

'One of the worst purchase decisions Andy ever made on the convertible currency markets. He exchanged a thousand herds of perfectly good South American llamas for two hundred harems.' The receptionist shook her head in despair. 'Now, we've any number of young, attractive, obedient, scantily clad virgins that nobody wants.'

'Appalling,' I concurred. 'Just out of interest, what price are they fetching?'

She again consulted the computer. 'Currently, one hundred pounds each.'

'I think it's important to diversify an investment portfolio.' I said. 'Perhaps it would be wise to buy some?'

'It's up to you, although there's significant volatility in the market. You could find their value plummets tomorrow, and your investment would be of no value for anything other than mindless, non stop sexual gratification.'

I watched others leaving the Bank with animals, cloth, jewels and spices from distant exotic lands, and I considered my options.

I counted out my bank notes. 'I'll have four virgins and an elephant, please,' I concluded.

That evening, I looked from my bedroom window to the parking space outside my flat where faithful Jumbo was settling down for the night. I then glanced at my bed where my remaining assets were safely stored.

I reflected on the benefits of wealth in tangible form and wondered how paper currency had ever caught on.

~*~*~*~*~

The Open Garden

George sat in the deckchair at his garden gate. He was about to count the money in his collecting tin when a male voice interrupted:

'Excuse me, is this one of the Open Gardens?'

'Yes,' replied George, glancing up at a middle-aged couple.

'Only you're not on the map of Open Gardens they gave us in the village.'

'No,' George agreed. 'I was a late entry, and there wasn't time to add me to any of the paperwork. It's just a pound each to look round,' he continued, lifting his tin.

His visitors contributed their admission fees, and George directed them to the rear of his bungalow.

He looked up and down the lane and saw no sign of other visitors. It was late in the afternoon and it was likely these would be the last. George painfully rose and limped to join his guests.

'It's rather different from other gardens we've seen today,' ventured his male visitor as George reached the couple.

'There aren't any plants,' noted the woman.

'The old arthritis stops me from doing too much gardening, these days,' George explained, 'so I went for a simple, low maintenance theme of just grass and SPIS.'

'SPIS?' queried the woman.

'Self Planting Indigenous Species.'

'You mean weeds?' she said.

'A weed is just a name for a plant growing in the wrong place,' replied George. 'My SPIS all carefully harmonise to construct a natural, uncultivated effect.'

'And the grass is three feet tall,' observed the man.

'I like to think that it forms a counterpoint juxtaposed to the manicured greenery, characteristic of the other exhibited gardens.'

The three looked out across the rusting mattress springs and other discarded household equipment, to the fire-gutted shell of an old motor car, beyond.

'I'm particularly pleased with that modern art installation,' announced George with pride. 'I may enter it for the Turner Prize.'

Before the couple could comment, the grass on the far side of the garden began to ripple, tracking the path of some hidden, approaching creature. The sound of growls and snarls reached their ears.

'Ah, that's Rufus, my Rottweiler,' said George. 'I don't know what's got into him today. He's bitten four of the visitors, and one had to be taken away by ambulance.'

George looked round to see his guests fleeing, panic-stricken, from the garden.

'They're serving tea and cakes in the Village Hall,' George helpfully shouted after them, before his voice was drowned-out by the savage barking of Rufus.

George sat down in his deckchair, and Rufus, having seen-off the intruders, laid quietly down on the ground beside him.

'Let's count the day's takings, boy,' George said to his companion. 'I reckon we've got over sixty quid here. That'll pay for getting all that rubbish taken away from the back garden.' He patted Rufus on the head. 'With any luck there'll be enough money left to have the grass cut and to get you a nice bone.'

~*~*~*~

The Housing Market

The house was too small for our uses.
It was now time to sell up and go.
Our two bedroomed terrace with no lawn at all
We now had begun to outgrow.

So onto the market our starter home went,
And buyers arrived to look round.
But none made an offer – so what could be wrong?
A way to sell had to be found.

A friend said the smell of some fresh baking bread
Would encourage the viewers to stay.
So we sprayed with a can of 'fresh baking bread' scent,
But the offers did not come our way.

A neighbour suggested the house was too full:
Our things were preventing a move.
So in storage we placed all possessions we owned,
Yet our luck didn't start to improve.

We next decorated both inside and out.
In new carpets we chose to invest.
We had a new kitchen and bathroom installed,
But did not spark the hoped interest.

My wife was appalled at now having to sleep
With each man when we thought we might sell.
I agreed that today's housing market was tough
As I serviced the gay ones as well.

We finally sold at a resonable price
Once the buyer had raised a large mortgage.
I don't think he actually wanted the house,
But some of his kin we held hostage.

Despite that, he drove a hard bargain.
We dropped by ten thousand or more.
He agreed on a compromise price, and we killed
Just one aunt and his brother-in-law.

So take note, you young couples who're selling.
Today's housing market is tough.
A couple of cans of 'fresh baking bread' scent
May simply not be enough.

~*~*~*~*~

April Showers

Derek looked out at the torrential rain from the window of his workshop. 'Let's have a beer,' he proposed, bending down and opening a hidden trapdoor in the floor. 'Mavis doesn't approve of alcohol,' Derek explained as he withdrew two cans from the camouflaged compartment and handed one to Peter.

'What the eye doesn't see, the heart doesn't grieve over, as they say,' Peter ventured.

'True enough, my friend.' Derek closed the trapdoor. 'This workshop's been a bit of a bolthole - Mavis seldom comes out here.'

Peter turned a page of his newspaper. 'Out of sight, out of mind, as they say.'

'So,' questioned Derek, changing the subject, 'what do you reckon for the three-thirty at Doncaster?'

Peter concluded his intense study of *The Racing Times*, closed the paper and placed it on the workbench. 'Live and Let Live,' he predicted decisively.

Derek slid open a secret drawer in his workbench, removed a mobile phone and dialled the local bookmaker. 'It's Derek Smith here. Twenty quid to win on Live and Let Live in the three-thirty at Doncaster, please.' Derek replaced the phone in its hideaway. 'Mavis doesn't approve of gambling,' he clarified in response to Peter's glance.

'One man's meat is another man's poison, as they say,' Peter responded sympathetically. 'Anyway, nothing ventured, nothing gained, as they say.'

'Mavis doesn't approve of TV, either,' said Derek as he pressed a concealed button in the ceiling. A television descended from an unsuspected recess. 'We can watch the race on this.'

They settled down to cheer on the selected nag. 'You can't teach an old dog new tricks, as they say,' sighed Peter, reflecting on Derek's wife.

Derek flicked a switch on his chair arm. A flap in the arm opened to reveal tobacco, tobacco papers, cigarettes, cigars and a lighter. 'Smoke?' he offered.

'Never look a gift horse in the mouth, as they say,' joked Peter, selecting a Havana.

'Mavis doesn't approve of smoking,' Derek lamented, rolling some Gold Leaf.

'You certainly need to mind your Ps and Qs, as they say.' Derek adjusted the volume on the remote. 'Too true, Peter.'

~**~

'That'll pay for some new supplies for the workshop,' declared a delighted Derek, twenty minutes later, as Live and Let Live romped across the line at odds of ten to one.

'Make hay while the sun shines, as they say,' encouraged Peter, also realising that the noise of rainfall on the roof had abated. He highlighted the latter fact by pointing upwards with his finger, and then he consulted his watch. 'Time and tide wait for no man, as they say,' Peter continued, rising from his chair.

Derek also stood up, moved to the window and surveyed the clearing sky. 'Yes, you'd best go before it pours again.' He opened a fanlight. 'This rain's a bit of a nuisance. Mind you,' he queried with a knowing smile, 'you know what they say about April showers?'

'I certainly do,' joked Peter, taking his meaning and returning a devilish wink. 'They say it's the best DVD of the series - better than *May Bathes* or even *June Takes a Sauna*!' The true significance of Derek's question suddenly dawned: 'You've got a copy haven't you, you old dog?'

Derek removed a wall panel to reveal his extensive collection of artistic magazines and DVDs. 'Keep it under your coat as you leave,' he cautioned, passing the disc to Peter, 'Mavis doesn't approve of pornography.'

'A nod's as good as a wink to a blind horse, as they say,' replied Peter in a conspiratorial tone.

Peter stepped from the workshop into the wet grass and felt the refreshing sprinkling of a final few raindrops. He looked at the droplets on his hands and then up at the passing clouds. 'They'll bring May flowers, as they say,' he remarked to himself as he crossed the lawn. 'Even Mavis would approve of that.'

~*~*~*~*~

The Girls' Get-together

'It's great to have these girls' get-togethers, don't you think?' said Janice as she topped-up the wine glasses of the other four wives.

'It certainly is,' responded Susan. 'It gives us a chance to talk about what we're really thinking about - the sorts of things that we can't discuss with our husbands.'

'Didn't I see you in Winchester on Friday?' said Alison to Julie, changing the subject.

'Yes, I was looking at some of those small terraced houses in Colebrook Street. If my husband, Alex, died, I think I'd move there. It would be so convenient for the shops and the theatres. What were you doing in Winchester?'

'Just shopping,' replied Alison. 'I bought a very nice dark red dress. I was thinking that, if George died, it would be ideal for me, as his widow, to wear at his funeral.'

'I often think about that when I buy clothes,' commented Celia. 'Of course a lot would depend on how Robert, my husband, passed on. Dark red would be perfect if he died peacefully in his sleep, but suppose he'd been run over by a combine harvester and torn limb from limb, or had been hacked apart by a deranged, machete wielding psychopath. If either happened, I think I might go for a darker shade of green, as the red would be a bit reminiscent of the blood and gore.'

'I agree totally,' said Janice. 'That was the very reason I didn't want to have a red car. It would have seemed so unsuitable if my other half, Henry, had been mashed to a pulp in an horrific motorway pile-up - particularly if he'd survived in agony until he had been cut from the wreckage. Mind you, I've had second thoughts about having now chosen a yellow one.'

'Why was that?' questioned Janice.

'Well, if he was dying of terminal liver cancer, he might turn yellow. If that happened, I think I'd have to sell the car, and then I'd lose a fortune as it's less than two years old.'

'It's definitely wise to plan ahead for these things,' ventured Susan. 'I liked the location of our house because you have to walk past the cemetery on the way to town. I thought that when my hubby, Chris, passed away, visiting his grave wouldn't take too much time out of the day.'

'All five of our husbands will be going on the Village Men's Group outing on Saturday,' Julie reminded them. 'I'd been thinking we should make a few provisional contingency plans in case the minibus is struck by lightning and then plummets from a motorway bridge into the path of a high speed train pulling tanks of aviation fuel.'

'What plans were you thinking of?' enquired Alison.

'Well, it occurred to me that the funerals would probably happen about this time next week, so we would have to postpone our weekly get-together.'

'Perhaps if we provisionally put the funerals in our diaries for Thursday and change our get-together to Wednesday?' suggested Susan.

'I've got a better idea,' proposed Celia. 'Why don't we postpone our get-together until Friday? We wouldn't have to worry about what time we got back then, as the men wouldn't be there.'

'Good plan,' they all agreed.

~*~*~*~*~

The NSSEUCYP

I am delighted to have been asked to speak at this conference of the 'National Society for the Support of English Upper Class Young People'. As a recipient of your generous help, I owe you all a very great debt of thanks.

Britain has a proud tradition of voluntary support groups for those marginalised by society. Single parents, the old, the disabled and refugees, to name just a few, enjoy practical help and emotional solace from myriad charities. There is a sector of our society, however, of which I am a part, which has been ignored by those seeking to better the lot of their fellow human beings.

I am young, physically and mentally well and extremely solvent due to inherited wealth and position. I can enjoy, therefore, the very best of an affluent western lifestyle. Frequently, however, I, and hundreds like me, are confronted with simple tasks of daily living which we are unable to undertake – simply because we cannot be bothered. This can cause huge practical problems in progressing with our lives, and yet our special needs have been cruelly overlooked. I felt totally abandoned until I was allocated a volunteer support worker from the NSSEUCYP.

She has been able to help me in many ways. When I cannot be bothered to get up in the morning, I know I can ring her and she will contact those with whom I have appointments. She will make excuses for me and even visit me at home to disable my alarm clock. On some evenings, I find it just too tedious to send out for food or turn on the TV. It is a great comfort to know that my support worker will call a take-away delivery service on my behalf or locate the TV remote. Only last Thursday, I could not be bothered to feed the cat and she was able to have Sheba put down for me.

The assistance provided by NSSEUCYP support workers has become a vital lifeline for many in this country. We must ask ourselves, however, why this has become necessary. What is it about modern society that makes so much of our daily routine just too tedious to contemplate? Clearly, for someone like myself, a normal lifestyle would involve getting up when I choose and having food, alcohol and entertainment permanently to hand. The government of this country has persistently failed, however, to develop an infrastructure to support this. The menial tasks which underpin such a lifestyle require large numbers of workers remunerated at nothing like the ridiculously high levels which employment law in this country dictates.

Our descent to our current dire position can, of course, be traced to William Wilberforce and those like him who opposed slave trading. The solution must be to reverse this trend and take the workers we require from sub-human species such as the Welsh, Scots and French – or even, indeed, our own English working class.

Well, that's all I can be bothered to contribute as I have suddenly had a desire to leave and fly to San Tropez. As I am supposed to be addressing you for around thirty minutes, however, I will now gratefully hand you over to my NSSEUCYP support worker.

~*~*~*~*~

Barking

As I walked with my dog on the common,
Another dog rushed up and barked.
His owner called 'Come back here, Benji,
We must go back to where we are parked.

'You mustn't keep barking at strangers
Or I'll leave you here all on your own.
And if you don't come back on calling,
You will not be getting a bone.'

The creature's command of the language
Must have surely been second to none,
And my mind drifted back to that crossword -
The one with one clue left undone.

I bent down to stroke him and posed him
The clue which had caused such vexation:
'An onomatopoeic expression
For canine vocalisation'.

You could see that the task was beneath him,
Eyes disparaging, rolling aloof.
But he swallowed his pride to assist me,
Condescendingly answering 'Woof'.

~*~*~*~

Sponsorship

I firmly believe that those of us who have been fortunate enough to attain any degree of affluence should have no hesitation in unstintingly giving to charitable causes. I had always taken this line, and had frequently given, whenever asked, with little thought about my donation.

It had come to my attention in recent years, however, that requests for a straightforward donation to a charity had become less frequent. More often, an individual had committed to undertake a specific task, and would be seeking sponsorship for its completion. The London Marathon was a fine case in point. Certainly, anyone who can *walk* twenty-six miles through London in the mid-summer heat, even if not dressed as a large furry animal, is welcome to my money for his or her cause.

Other sponsored tasks, however, gave me cause to reflect. I sponsored a work colleague who was planning to walk the Great Wall of China, and then another who was planning to visit the great Aztec and Inca monuments of South America. I must make it clear that, in both cases, all the donated money went to the nominated charities, and the individuals concerned paid their own expenses. Nevertheless, they were clearly being sponsored for having a good time and doing what they would have done anyway, without sponsorship. This realisation led to two major changes in my charitable donation strategy.

The first was that I now only sponsor those who are doing something that they do not want to do. There is, therefore, an element of sacrifice involved. This caused requests for sponsorship to significantly reduce initially, until friends and colleagues began to think it through. I am now proud to have sponsored Jones from Finance for having his mother-in-law stay for a week. Janice in Sales has raised nearly two hundred pounds for Great Ormond Street by regularly visiting her old and disabled, though cantankerous and vitriolic, aunt. Also, Mavis in Despatch has gained nearly one thousand pounds for the National Heart Foundation by agreeing to have sex with her rather boring but nevertheless kindly husband at least once every two months.

The second change is my own venture into sponsored activities for charity. I was delighted to raise nearly five hundred pounds from my sponsored affair with Sally from the Stationery Department. Our target of intercourse twenty-five times in a week was challenging, but thoughts of the desperate need of earthquake victims in Asia drove us onwards to success. My recent sponsored tour of the Greek islands was also extremely lucrative for Oxfam, especially with the bonus of ten pence from each sponsor for every whole bottle of Retzina consumed.

I am painfully aware, however, that the above contributions are but a drop in the ocean compared to the massive need for humanitarian funding. This is why I am now writing to young actresses, alcohol manufacturers and drug suppliers, worldwide, to gain support for my proposed, sponsored 'sexdrugsandboozeathon'. It is undoubtedly an ambitious target to have sexual intercourse with a constant stream of the world's most desirable women whilst consuming prodigious quantities of alcohol and drugs. A simple viewing of any evening news programme, however, underlines the ubiquitousness of poverty and suffering. I believe, therefore, that this is the very least I can do.

~*~*~*~

The Man who fell to Earth

A loud bang, sudden unexpected motion and intense cold wrenched Lance from sleep.

He could not have known that failure of a pressure bulkhead in the ageing airliner, just minutes before touchdown at Southampton Airport, had ripped a hole in the fuselage adjacent to his seat. He knew, however, that seconds previously he had been inside an aircraft, and now he was in the open air and tumbling earthwards.

Having recently undertaken a charity parachute jump, he instinctively spread his arms and legs and arched his back to effect a stable, face down descent.

It was a clear, summer afternoon, and the familiar topography of Southern Hampshire lay below him like Google Earth.

Autobiographical highlights flashed before his eyes: There, in this vision, was Gwen. She had captured his heart since they had first sat together in Miss Watson's class at primary school. She dreamed, however, of fairy-tale romance, and, despite resolute attempts to win her hand, Lance had never matched Gwen's naïve, chivalric aspirations. Despite that, he loved her passionately.

Suddenly, the face of Oswald Mordred entered the vision. His massive wealth and superficial charm had enchanted Gwen to conclude that Oswald was her prince. To Lance's despair, Gwen and Oswald had married after a whirlwind romance.

Gwen had soon learned, however, of Oswald's unfaithfulness, and she now felt as if trapped atop a loveless, though materially comfortable, castle tower - awaiting rescue.

Lance looked down upon the Hamble estuary where Oswald's luxury yacht, 'Oswald's Kingdom', was moored. An unnatural calm descended upon him as a plan formed in his mind – finally, he could prove his undying love for the fair Gwen. He spread his coat and noted with satisfaction that he could retard his descent and effect sideways motion.

Henry Johnson from Winchester fell past. Lance recalled him as the passenger who had occupied the seat next to his. Lance waved, but Henry seemed, somehow, preoccupied.

Returning to his quest, Lance banked to the right and set course for Hamble Marina. He calculated that, travelling at two hundred miles per hour, he should, in the finest Kamikaze and Exocet traditions, be able to sink 'Oswald's Kingdom'. Lance knew that Gwen was away, so could not be on board. It was Saturday afternoon, however, and Oswald almost certainly would be.

Lance flew onwards. Eric Robinson from Andover and Albert Henderson from Basingstoke dropped past, having delegated their plans to gravity. Lance identified the flight crew of the budget airline by the logos on their parachutes.

At last, his target came into clear view, and he prepared for his final approach…

~**~

Six months later, Gwen jumped, with a parachute, from a Cessna over Southampton. She wished to experience the manner in which Lance had executed his last heroic and romantic act as he had sunk 'Oswald's Kingdom' with the loss of Oswald and two of his many mistresses.

Gwen had inherited Oswald's wealth. Looking down upon Hamble Marina, she sighted her newly commissioned luxury yacht at the mooring once occupied by 'Oswald's Kingdom'.

There had been no finer hero after whom to name it – someone who had, at last, met her romantic ideals. Gwenevere would forever be reminded of his passion and valour as she sailed on 'Lancelot of the Skies'.

~*~*~*~*~

French Comprehension

'When is the next bus to Paris?' I asked an elderly Frenchman who was sitting at the bus stop.

'Comment?'

'When le next bus à Paris?' I translated with increased volume in a stereotypical French accent.

'Pardon monsieur, je ne comprends pas.' He turned and called to a man across the street. 'Pierre, comprenez-vous cet homme de l'Angleterre?'

Pierre joined us.

'Hello Pierre,' I said, 'when is the next bus to Paris?'

Pierre shook his head. 'Non René, je ne lui comprends pas aussi,' he conceded.

'*Bus*,' I stressed, drawing the shape of such a vehicle in the air with my index fingers.

'Je pense que c'est un film, René, n'est-ce pas?' ventured Pierre.

'Non, Non,' replied René, 'Je pense que c'est un livre.'

Encouraged by their efforts to understand, I mimed the doors of a bus opening followed by my boarding of the bus, my paying of the conductor and then finally my alighting in central Paris – the latter being rather cleverly illustrated, I thought, by standing with my legs wide apart with arms raised above my head and fingertips touching in perfect resemblance of the Eiffel Tower.

'C'est peut-être un ballet?' suggested Pierre.

'Non,' responded René, 'il doit être un livre ou un film ou une émission de télévision.'

We were joined by a large, bearded man. 'Och Aye it's hot,' he said, sitting down and wiping his brow.

'You speak English,' I said to the new arrival with relief.

'Ah prefer tae hink ay it as Scottish,' he replied in a heavy Glaswegian accent. He turned to the Frenchmen. 'Dae ye ken th' time ay th' next wee bus tae Paris?'

'Oui monsieur,' René answered, 'le bus arrive en cinq minutes.' René raised a palm with fingers spread to confirm the number five.

'Cheers mun,' said the Scotsman.

'You understood him?' I said to René in amazement.

'Comment?'

I pointed to the Scotsman and then my mouth and then my ear.

'Je suis certain que c'est un film,' proclaimed Pierre. 'Est-il "Braveheart"?'

'Bien sûr, ce film est sur le thème de les grands Écossais et les Anglais stupide,' noted René.

'Ah hink it's yer accent,' suggested the Scotsman. 'Tae be frenk, Ah hud tae kin' ay guess whit ye waur sayin', myself.'

'But I speak with a very neutral southern English accent,' I protested.

'Yah sassenach disnae hae mony common pronunciations wi' other languages an' dialects,' he continued. 'Tak' th' way Ah say "bus". It soonds jist loch th' way th' French say "bus". Ye say "baas". Soonds loch naethin' but a wee lamb lookin' fur its maw.'

This Celtic Professor Higgins was about to expand further on these finer points of linguistic difference when the Paris bus arrived. He and René climbed aboard.

I was about to follow when Pierre tapped me on the shoulder. 'Excuse-moi, monsieur,' he said, 'est-ce que le film est "Braveheart"?'

~*~*~*~*~

The National Society for Opposition to Everything
Chair's Report

As Chair of The National Society for Opposition to Everything (NSFOTE), I am delighted to report on another successful year.

The Society has long campaigned to prevent anyone from doing anything, and now that we have so many members in influential positions and at grass roots in Britain, we have been able to pursue our objectives on multiple fronts.

The power industry has been particularly affected this year with successful campaigns against the use of fossil and nuclear fuels. Local opposition to wind turbines across the land led, in 2009, to the closure of the Vesta wind turbine factory on the Isle of Wight, and efforts continue to thwart plans for tidal, solar and other forms of renewable energy based on any half-baked rationale. Impact on the scenery or on some obscure species of local wildlife remain popular objections.

We hope that by 2050 no power of any kind will be able to be generated in the United Kingdom.

Infiltration of planning committees by our members continues to prevent the construction of new buildings and stop existing structures from being modified or demolished. The rise in the number of families unable to locate affordable homes is heartening testimony to this success. This victory is all the more rewarding in locations where it is the local population themselves who have campaigned against low cost housing for local people.

Such actions have, of course, been greatly assisted by planning committees that have made every derelict structure a listed building to avoid any constructive use of it or its site.

The engagement of local NIMBY movements has significantly aided our cause. They have selflessly opposed not just housing but mobile phone masts, power lines, new shops, supermarkets and many other such projects. This is despite enduring overcrowding, poor local communications, power cuts and the need to drive miles to find a decent shop. The NSFOTE says well done to one and all!

Opposition to the closure of local pubs, shops and post offices has also been selflessly pursued by many who have never used these local amenities and plan never to do so. A special mention is deserved for their efforts.

These local NIMBY groups have developed fast response strategies such as the manufacture of half completed signs, posters, leaflets and petitions with headings such as *'Join Our Opposition To …'* or *'No … Here!'* - each having a space to allow rapid addition of their demonised project of the week. Other signs simply say *'Down with the proposal!!!'* so they can be quickly deployed in any circumstance.

As many of you know, I am standing down as Chair due to opposition to my chairmanship in the past twelve months. I wish to assure the new incumbent that he or she can count on myself and other members of the NSFOTE to stir up unrest, argue every trivial point and raise irrational objections to any proposal he or she might make. Thus I hope we can continue to avoid any progress in the spirit of the glorious history of our Society.

A Whinger
Chair
The National Society for Opposition to Everything

~*~*~*~*~

5 – Food and Drink

A Brakspearean Sonnet

From St. Louis to tour England I came.
Our trip was brief; the coach kept on the go.
In Stratford, houses stood of special fame,
Though their significance I still don't know.
Anne Hathaway's was one we drove on past,
Then Mary Arden's home came into view.
I think our guide said Brakspear's was the last.
Who all these people were, I never knew.
Brakspear, I later learned, brewed English beers.
A stop for lunch at his small pub was planned.
The taste of one drawn pint confirmed my fears:
'Twas warm and flat like ales in all England!
The Brits should visit my home town to see
Real beer at the Budweiser Brewery.

~**~

Footnotes:
1 - Stratford upon Avon, England, was the birthplace and home of William Shakespeare.
2 - Anne Hathaway was the wife of William Shakespeare.
3 - Mary Arden was the mother of William Shakespeare.
4 - Brakspear is an English brewer. The modern brewery is in Witney, Oxfordshire. Witney is just forty miles from Stratford upon Avon, and the Brakspear Brewery supplies to pubs in that area.
5 - The original Budweiser Brewery is in St. Louis, Missouri, USA.
6 - The poetic form above is a Shakespearean, or English sonnet. This consists of fourteen lines, each containing ten syllables. Each line is written in iambic pentameter which is a pattern of an unstressed syllable followed by a stressed syllable, repeated five times. The rhyme scheme is ABAB CDCD EFEF GG in which the last two lines are a rhyming couplet.
7 - William Shakespeare wrote 154 sonnets.
8 - In 1557 John Shakespeare, the father of William Shakespeare, obtained Public Office when he was elected as ale-taster of the Borough of Stratford.

~*~*~*~

You Are What You Eat

Members of the jury, as judge presiding in relation to this trial, it is now my task to sum up the case for the defence before you retire to consider your verdict.

There is no doubt about the circumstances that led to the demise of Mr Romano 'Spud' Wilja, nor that his demise was due to the deliberate actions of his wife. The question you must decide upon is whether she is guilty of murder.

You will recall that exhibit A was a photograph of flamingos. The defence pointed out that the pink colouration of their feathers was not an inherent characteristic but due to pigmentation absorbed from the creatures on which they fed. The defence then reminded you that there was much tribal folklore based on the premise that the characteristics of an animal would be assumed by those who consumed it. The courage of a lion, for example, might be gained by eating the heart of a lion. Expert witnesses then testified that there was a scientific basis to such beliefs. Indeed it had been proven that food we consumed could alter the very genetic structure of our cells.

The life history of Mr Wilja was then related. You heard of his habitual inactivity and his prodigious consumption of chips, crisps, waffles and other potato-based food products. The defence thus contended that the genetic profile of Mr Wilja had become modified to the extent that his proper biological classification should be that of a potato.

The defence acknowledged that his wife had immersed him in boiling water, skinned him, sliced him, plunged those slices into a deep fat fryer and then eaten them. They challenged the assertion of the prosecution, however, that this constituted torture and cannibalism of a most bizarre and psychotic nature. They contended that her actions were, in fact, the entirely normal behaviour of any cook.

In addition, the defence went on to examine the genetic characteristics of Mrs Wilja. It was reported that she had developed a passion for chocolate from an early age and that her DNA profile had thus become indistinguishable from that of a bar of chocolate. In this context you were reminded that there was no legislation which governed the behaviour of confectionery towards stem tubers.

If you decide that a heinous crime has been committed against Mr Wilja, then you must find his wife guilty of murder. If, however, you accept the genetic modification argument, then you might like to join me in my office for elevenses, as I understand that the clerk of the court, having had a life long penchant for cocoa and biscuits, is now officially categorised as a chocolate digestive.

~*~*~*~*~

What's the Damage, Squire?

Me, me family an' me mates like nothin' better than a really good party.

This used to cause loads o' grief. Just last year, we took over our local pub, the Risin' Sun, for a bash. The customers and staff kept complainin' about the noise, the excessive drinkin', the rowdiness, the assaults, the rapes, the murders, the arson and so on. It took a lot o' fun out o' the do. It was only next mornin', as I stood with the owner lookin' at the smolderin' remains o' the pub buildin', that a better plan for future parties was 'atched between us.

We ain't short o' a bob or two, although the pub owner was a bit surprised when I got out me wad and slipped 'im a million in fifties to pay for the party and rebuild the pub. 'e was more surprised when I asked for a bookin' for next year - when 'e'd got the place more to rights, like. After a bit o' thought, he accepted. It would pay more to build a new place just for our party than it would to run it is as a pub and restaurant for a year.

Buildin' specifically to purpose allowed a number of innovative features. As they only needed usin' for one night, chairs could be robust enough to sit on, but break easily when smashed over someone's 'ed. Windows could be made of theatrical glass so there was no unnecessary arteries severed by those thrown through 'em. There was time to recruit ex SAS soldiers as waiters and bar staff and issue 'em with kevlar clothin' to protect 'em from most o' the knives and stray bullets.

After a small cash contribution to the Chief Constable's retirement fund, the police even agreed to evacuate an' cordon off the 'alf-mile surrounding the pub on the night o' the party.

On the night, I first thought that the kevlar protection for the staff 'ad been a mistake when me mates kept callin' 'em all 'Kev'. Pissin'-off ex

SAS men, 'owever, just led to 'em wadin' into the fights too, so that was loads better than last year when the staff were really borin' and just cowered in a corner and prayed.

One great plan was the buildin' of a swimmin' pool and fillin' it with punch. Even them what drowned 'ad a fantastic night.

I admit it might 'av been a mistake to store all the fireworks for our 'uge, planned display in the smokin' area o' the pub. Still, people got to see the display,,close up, without 'avin' to go out in the cold. Also it gave the local emergency services a chance to test their Major Civil Emergency Plan.

All in all, this year, it was f**kin' brilliant. The do was just last night and the landlord's already got some JCBs in to fill the crater so work can begin on rebuildin' the pub for next year.

~*~*~*~*~

The Human Liberation Movement

Jo Jo looked down from the rainforest canopy. He checked lower branches for all members of his chimpanzee troop. As alpha male, he took his responsibility for troop welfare very seriously.

He glanced at the human compound, far below. He noted the lavish facilities: the swimming pools, the saunas and myriad serving staff. He also sensed the heavy air of sadness and foreboding that had been intensifying during past weeks.

Jo Jo recalled that atmosphere five years ago, just before all compound occupants had left and been replaced by excited and joyous newcomers.

Curiosity had led him then to follow the wagons transporting the earlier residents away.

He had been horrified and sickened - they were taken to an abattoir and killed.

Viewers of BBC wildlife documentaries retain two misapprehensions about chimpanzees:

The first is that they are not very bright. It is true they lack the evolutionary advantages of some cerebral functions - such as advanced speech. Nevertheless, they possess a level of intelligence and reasoning which is easily superior to that, for example, of backbench politicians.

The second misapprehension is that chimpanzees are violent killers. Jo Jo lamented the dreadful publicity his species had received following David Attenborough's film of a troop killing a monkey. Jo Jo had known Ca Ca, the leader of that troop. He had been a dangerous psychopath since chimphood. For Attenborough to conclude all chimpanzees acted in that way was like citing Hitler's behaviour as typical of humans. Jo Jo, and most of his kind, were peaceable vegetarians.

Following the human massacre, Jo Jo frequented the compound, listening to conversation snippets from the new arrivals. He had learned the rudiments of English from the BBC World Service on a wind-up radio dropped by an eco-tourist.

Jo Jo gradually understood: An English broadcaster, Hugh Fearnley-Whittingstall, had asserted that humans made a contract with farm animals. Humans ate the animals, but fulfilled their contractual responsibilities by caring well for the creatures during their lives.

Vegetarian animal rights lawyers had argued this was an invalid contract, as the animals could not exercise informed choice. It was concluded, however, that it was reasonable to eat volunteer humans in exchange for a five-year period of unstinting excess.

The commercial value of the delicacy easily funded development of secluded luxury holiday farms.

The desperate and disadvantaged volunteered in droves. During the first four years, they lived their perceptions of Heaven on Earth. As the end of the fifth approached, however, the ghoulish consequences of their Faustian pacts took form.

Jo Jo was unimpressed by contracts. He abhorred killing or violence towards any creature. He had formed the Human Liberation Movement.

Jo Jo had, however, heard radio recordings of Dr Martin Luther King Jnr and had profoundly understood the relationship between 'peaceful ends' and 'peaceful means' – something, he reflected, that some humans in similar movements had tragically overlooked.

Jo Jo's call transformed the hush of the evening rainforest into a kaleidoscope of noise and action. Hundreds of chimpanzees converged on the human compound, tearing down fences and gates. The reprieved took control and began to plan their freedom.

Peace returned to the rainforest. Jo Jo and the troop rested briefly before moving on. They would reach the next compound by dawn.

~*~*~*~

Chicken

'Dinner is served,' announced Derek to his two guests.

'Excellent,' replied George as he and Alison arose from the sofa and began to walk to the dining room.

'It's chicken,' said Susan as the two couples sat down at the dining table. 'I hope that's OK?'

'Just as long as it's free range,' said George, earnestly.

'I've got all the documentation,' Susan confirmed, reaching for a folder from the breakfast bar. 'Her name was Esmeralda. She enjoyed the highest standards of rearing.' Susan removed a photograph from the folder and passed it to George. 'This is a picture from one of her holidays in Tenerife. She was also a personal friend of Jamie Oliver.'

'Free range chickens are pretty expensive, though,' reflected Alison. 'Do you mind if I ask how much you paid for Esmeralda?'

'Eight hundred and ninety-seven pounds,' Susan replied, 'although that included delivery and her pre-slaughter counselling.' Susan looked puzzled for a moment and then turned to Alison. 'If you usually bought free range chickens, you would have known the cost.'

There was a short, embarrassed silence.

'You don't buy free range, do you?' challenged Susan.

Alison and George glanced at each other. In an instant they silently debated whether to confess to their oldest friends, and agreed that pretence was impossible.

'It's worse that that,' revealed George, avoiding eye contact with his hosts. 'We buy the super-cheap chickens.'

'Super-cheap chickens?' enquired Derek.

'Chickens that are reared to the very highest standards cost as much as second-hand cars,' George explained. 'Intensively, but less humanely, reared fowl can be bought for a few pounds.' He looked at Alison. 'The prices really plummet when the birds have been,' he restrained the increasing enthusiasm in his voice, 'well... punished.'

Susan broke the ensuing silence: 'Why would anyone punish a chicken?'

'Do you have the Internet?' responded Alison.

'Yes,' replied Derek.

'Do you ever look at the S and M chicken sites?' continued Alison.

'What's S and M?' said Derek.

'Well, it's like when you're spanking Susan,' George replied absentmindedly.

Susan blushed and glared at Derek.

Derek and Alison glared at George.

Dinner was postponed as all four retired to the computer.

Derek and Susan looked on in amazement as disobedient chickens at *naughtychickens.com* received the mild though humiliating discipline they so justly deserved.

'Some sites are more hard core, but we're not into that sort of thing,' explained George. 'There are lots of sites out there. Most sell off the chickens really cheaply when they've finished with them.'

'They'll usually despatch them to your door, oven ready,' added Alison.

Derek and Susan were initially appalled but, at the same time, felt strangely aroused.

Both were aware that some of the excitement had gone from their bedroom activities and that new inspiration was needed. The presence of their friends and the third bottle of wine somehow legitimised admission of their most secret and guarded fantasies about *Gallus domesticus*.

Also, Coq au vin would never again require a second mortgage.

~*~*~*~

Preparing for Christmas

The secret of a successful Christmas is careful planning.

I commenced Christmas preparations in July when I arranged to have a letter sent to my relatives informing them of my death. To avoid funeral attendance, the letter explained that I had succumbed to salmonella on a cross channel ferry and, for health and safety reasons, had been buried at sea.

This forestalled receipt of family Christmas cards, particularly those containing long, tedious, duplicated, personal chronologies of the year. It also excused me effort and expense on reciprocal Yuletide greetings. Critically, however, it prevented any possibility of an invitation to spend Christmas day with family members.

As a pensioner living alone, invitations to be subjected to this annual, charitable, Christian ordeal are an ever present danger. This is particularly true in my village where residents seem to have sworn a solemn oath that no person who lives alone shall ever have a nice, peaceful Christmas day.

It was to address this diabolic covenant that, from November, I began to inform neighbours that I would be spending Christmas one hundred miles away with my, nonexistent, Cousin Eric. Unfortunately, John and Mavis live in the adjoining semi, and sound passing through the connecting wall would have made it impossible to remain at home without their awareness.

John and Mavis are elderly and might not live much longer, so I initially considered hastening their demise. I concluded, however, that this would be fraught with difficulties: It would have to be executed at the last moment to avoid the possibility of new tenants arriving before Christmas. I also feared that, due to my lack of homicide experience, the police might be more than a match for my cunning. Finally, upon reflection, murdering one's neighbours seemed somewhat contrary to the Christmas spirit.

Fortunately, these neighbours have a daughter in Australia who they had not seen for five years. The daughter was very grateful for my letter about the declining heath of her parents and the suggestion that this might be the last opportunity to fly them to Australia for Christmas.

John and Mavis were delighted at this invitation, although unfortunately became aware of my part in its planning. They thanked me profusely and insisted that I join them for Christmas dinner next year. At least I have twelve months to carefully revisit my original plan.

So came Christmas Eve. I placed in my windows the life-sized photographs of my deserted rooms. I then reconstructed my living room in the back bedroom. In the fading light, I loaded a suitcase into my car and waved to several neighbours as I drove away.

The lock-up garage is just two miles away, so I soon concealed the car, donned my black tracksuit and balaclava and returned home along footpaths.

Today is Christmas day. I got up late and didn't bother to dress. I've had a brilliant traditional Christmas dinner with all the trimmings but no effort due to Marks and Spencers and the microwave. I'll wash up in February.

Now it's time for the Queen's speech. I won't watch that tedious crap, of course. I think I'll open my second wine box, have a fag and surf some more pornography on the Internet.

Christmas is wonderful and need not be stressful. It's all a question of planning.

~*~*~*~

Indemnity

Dear John and Sheila,

Rachael and I are delighted to hear that you're finally planning to visit England after so many years abroad.

We're very glad that you'll both be able to have dinner with us next month.

Before you arrive, you need to know about some changes in UK law since you last joined us for a dinner party.

You might have read in the UK newspapers about a rise in the number of guests suing hosts for accidental injuries caused during social visits. It's now obligatory for visitors to sign a disclaimer stating that they accept full responsibility for any trauma, physical or psychological, which may befall them.

We enclose two copies of the disclaimer form. Please sign one each, have them witnessed and return them to us at least fourteen days before your arrival so they can be registered with our solicitor.

Unfortunately, these disclaimers have sometimes been challenged in court. In a landmark case, a visitor to a coffee morning successfully sued her host for causing Post Traumatic Stress Disorder by revealing her husband's marital infidelity. Public liability insurance is now required by anyone who plans to entertain social visitors.

As you'll only be with us from 7.00 pm until midnight, we're able to insure at only twenty pounds for the evening. It's become etiquette for such costs to be divided between host and guest, so we hope you won't mind enclosing a cheque for ten pounds when you return the above papers.

Also, please don't be offended if we insist that you are off the premises before the cover lapses at midnight. It's OK to carry on our conversation in the street.

I think we mentioned in our previous letter that we've been decorating Sophie's bedroom. Regrettably, we're not going to have time to finish painting the skirting boards before you arrive. This means that her room remains officially designated as a 'construction site' and 'hard hat' area, and so we won't be able to show you the work we've done. In part that's because we don't have extra sets of protective clothing and equipment, but in any case a viewing would significantly raise the insurance cost.

I'm afraid that this designation also applies to the garden due to the water feature we're building. We're taking photographs for you of these areas and other parts of the house that the Law prevents you from visiting.

By the way, we hope it's OK to have a pre-packed salad for dinner? Rachael hasn't fully completed the relevant food hygiene certificates, and the insurance indemnity in relation to food poisoning requires this. In fact, until she's properly certified, she's not legally allowed to re-enter our kitchen.

Finally, the insurance company insists that contemporaneous notes are kept of any conversations and activities undertaken with guests while on the premises. I gather this is so antecedents of events for which there might be a claim can, if necessary, be accurately reported in court.

Minute takers are in demand for this sort of thing at the moment, particularly on Saturday nights, and so, if we can't get one, we wondered if Sheila, with her secretarial experience, could take the minutes of our evening?

Anyway, we look forward to seeing you soon.

Love,

Henry and Rachael.

~*~*~*~*~

The Boozer Laureate

To post of Poet Laureate I came,
To frame the Nation's thoughts in clever verse.
In Britain, mine's a role of modest fame,
The other laureate, he fares much worse.
Drowned sorrows are not regal for a Queen,
The Boozer Laureate fulfils this role.
When sadness might the Monarch's state demean,
His glass, vicarious, must her console.
Think of this Drinking Laureate as he
Gets rat-arsed for her Royal Majesty.

In ninety-two the BL's skills seemed fit,
Sarah and Andrew, their own ways embark.
Dom Per-i-gnon White Gold, the BL hit,
Then through came the divorce of Anne and Mark.
Old Windsor Castle burned with yellow flame;
Di-a-na, her True Stor-y was renowned;
The split of Charles and Di then shortly came -
Pernod-Ricard Per-ri-er-Jouet, downed.
The BL stayed loy-al-ly on the piss.
The Queen survived An-nus Hor-ri-bi-lis.

Deep in the Palace cellars, on his knees,
The BL, for the Monarch, slumps, stone drunk.
As Philip insults foreign dignitaries,
Methuselas of Cristal Brut are sunk.
When Di died, Krug was shipped in by the crate.
Such selfless dedication we forget.
Official secrets, BLs can't relate,
Though Her Majesty recalls her debt.
A knighthood in the Honours he might see
For Queen and the French Champagne industry.

~*~*~*~*~

6 – Advertising and the Media

LaunchOLift

As senior scientist at NASA's rocket propulsion laboratory, Meg knew that the science and technology of chemically powered rocket engines had reached a ceiling. To attain the velocities and fuel storage required for inter-stellar travel, new propulsion systems would inevitably seem to be required; perhaps ion technology; perhaps even warp drives?

Meg was pondering this problem as she shopped for cosmetics.

She was casually reading the label on a tub of moisturising cream when, suddenly, two facts became dramatically apparent: Firstly, the names of the chemicals contained in the product were unfamiliar, despite her two doctorates in chemistry. Secondly, the cream possessed astounding properties. It appeared that it could not only reverse the ageing process, but also make its users physically indistinguishable from leading international models.

Meg realised that there could be just one explanation: The cosmetics company had employed the greatest scientists of all time who had, in their secret laboratories, advanced the frontiers of chemistry by decades, if not centuries.

On returning to her lab, Meg rang the cosmetics giant and proposed collaboration with NASA.

The company agreed to help, although insisted that any formulae for their rocket enhancement products would be commercial secrets that could not be shared with NASA.

So it was that packs of LaunchOLift arrived at the lab. The promotional video that accompanied them was impressive. It explained, using glamorous models, how natural ingredients, including new formula, organic BlastOff Pro 49C, guaranteed that even a rusted bucket would experience no problems in reaching Mars.

The gel was carefully applied to a rocket engine on the test rig. Inexplicably, however, it demonstrated no increased performance.

Scientists from the cosmetics company considered the problem and soon provided new LaunchOLift VT10, enriched with AntiGravitol QA. This was even supplied with a convenient applicator. Once again, however, there was no discernable effect.

Meg thought back to the promotional video. The use of LaunchOLift had definitely made her feel better about her project. Perhaps there had been some physical improvements that the test equipment could not detect?

The NASA resource committee had exhibited a typically male attitude. They had decided that no further funds could be allocated to rocket enhancement cosmetics without some demonstrable scientific evidence of their efficacy.

On balance, Meg saw this as a loss to NASA. After all, the Ferrari Formula One Team seemed to be showing significant success following collaboration with the same cosmetics company. Their cars were now routinely treated with new formula, organic SpeedATrack 27J, enriched with CornerFast BL94.

Dee Caffari had entered the record books in February 2009 as the first woman to sail solo around the world in both directions. How might she have fared, Meg wondered, had her boat not received liberal applications of WaveSuppress M76, enriched with herbal essences including StormOStop ZR 21?

Meg inspected the engine on the test rig. For now, she would have to intensify research into those warp drives - propulsion systems that involved the controlled distortion of space-time, manipulating the underlying fabric of the Universe.

That certainly involved exciting scientific concepts, if not quite as advanced as those claimed for LaunchOLift and its sister products.

~*~*~*~*~

The Product

Those of us in the High Street retail trade had greatly feared the Internet. For years, customers had believed that they were visiting shops to purchase items they wished to buy. Few realised that they were really buying what we chose to sell them.

Some of us believed that bookshops were taking this idea to absurd lengths. We worried that the public were bound to detect something odd in the fact that there were millions of books which readers might wish to own, but that book-sellers, nationwide, tended to promote only six at a time – three of which were cookbooks by celebrity chefs.

We decided to commission a survey to understand why customers kept returning to shops despite the fact that they could get infinitely greater choice and enormously better value on the Internet.

The results were very encouraging. They revealed that consumers fell into three groups:

Approximately one third realised that shops were a dismally poor way to obtain goods and stayed at home in front of their computers.

A further third were products of British late twentieth century education so lacked the reasoning, literacy and numeracy skills to detect the problem.

The final third simply enjoyed shopping so much that what they purchased was virtually immaterial.

This revelation led to a revolution in High Street retail strategy. Shops began to stock increasingly restricted ranges at increasingly exorbitant prices. The outcome was exactly as predicted by the research: Sales fluctuated but never fell below a certain level as the latter two groups simply carried on shopping, regardless.

This strategy was so successful that The Federation of High Street Retailers finally decided to pursue the approach to its ultimate conclusion and sell just one product in all shops.

There was initially some debate as to what The Product should be. Consumer research showed clearly that it would need to be environmentally friendly and thus biodegradable. This did not resolve, however, the dilemma of which of millions of potential items should be chosen.

The breakthrough came with the concept of a pre-biodegraded Product. Consumers could then be confident that that their purchase would have no ecological impact as it would have biodegraded to the point of non-existence prior to purchase. Also, as nothing remained of The Product, the question of what it had once been became somewhat academic.

The Biodegrading-To-Non-Existence or BTNE process increased manufacturing costs, but the modern consumer was now happy to pay for ecological peace of mind.

Sales and consumer satisfaction were high and all seemed to be going well when scandal rocked the High Street retail trade to its foundations.

Due to cheaper labour costs, Products had been manufactured in China and the Far East. Undercover journalists discovered that such imports had not been pre-biodegraded. Instead, non-existent Products had been substituted, indistinguishable from authentic merchandise.

This led to worrying times but ultimately was a boon for the British economy as shoppers were prepared to pay even higher prices for a quality checked and certified local pre-biodegraded Product.

I now feel confident that the future of High Street retailing is assured.

Guarantee of humane production methods has even attracted the endorsement of those celebrity chefs.

~*~*~*~*~

Media Song 893

Our rock band, *The Crap*, wasn't doing well. None of us were particularly musical - we couldn't sing, and we were pretty useless on the instruments. Also, we were drunk or stoned most of the time - something that improved performances from our perspective but apparently not from the standpoint of audiences. In all the above respects, however, we were very similar to many other leading bands, and so our lack of success remained puzzling.

It was whilst throwing up over the side of a cross channel ferry after a particularly challenging drinking session in rough seas that our crucial weakness suddenly became clear to me. It was our lyrics.

Sailing by *Rod Stewart* was enjoying its thousandth rendition of the crossing and, indeed, may have contributed to my nausea. Clearly a lucky set of lyrics had caused P&O to rescue Rod from obscurity. I reflected that, similarly, members of *Slade* would have faded into the quiet anonymity of a nursing home had *Merry Christmas* not generated annual royalties from every shopping mall in the land. Also, *Cliff Richard* might now be eking out an impoverished retirement from the meagre residual royalties of *Bachelor Boy* if it had not been for the legal requirement in the UK to play *Congratulations* at every celebration party. Virtually any song with references to the weather had kept its writers, performers and their heirs in clover for generations.

As lyricist for *The Crap*, my songs had, thus far, been very conventional: Boy meets girl; boy gets girl pregnant; girl takes boy to court for maintenance etc. It was clear that I must now compose media friendly songs. Songs that made no sense but contained collections of random, topical words and phrases that could be used by the media in as many contemporary contexts as possible. Perhaps one day P&O would even replace 'I am sailing, I am sailing' with 'I am throwing up, I am throwing up'!

The rest is history.

The *Crapsongs* record label has given its kind consent for the publication below of the lyrics and guitar chords of one of *The Crap's* greatest Number Ones, *Media Song 893*.

Those of you who have crossed the channel by ferry at Christmas will be more than familiar with the final words of this song which are now played repeatedly over ferry PA systems during the festive season as the successor to *Sailing*.

The backing for *Media Song 893* was, of course, originally provided by the Royal Philharmonic Orchestra; The Massed Bands of the British Army, Navy and Air Force, and four Welsh male voice choirs. For karaoke fans, however, we sobered up our lead guitarist long enough for him to record an acoustic twelve string version of the tune which you can download as an MP3 from *the Short Humour Site* at *www.short-humour.org.uk..*

Why not sing along when next at your computer?

Media Song 1 to *Media Song 6578* are available from *Crapsongs Music*. All helpfully utilise the same tune as *Media Song 893* which has saved the band hours in rehearsal time.

~**~

Media Song 893

by The Crap

Guitar Chords:

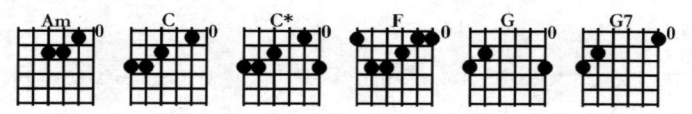

    Am   C   C*   F   G   G7

```
       C              G           Am         C
This is a song for me; it's a song for you;
       F                        G7
It's a song for the animals in the zoo.
       C              G           Am       C
It's a song for the leaders of the Earth;
       F                           G7
It's a song for the poor with commercial worth.

          C        C*        F           Am         G7
Spare a thought for the old folk, pensions cut,
          C C*F        Am      G7
With the N H S in a total rut.

                    **********

          C             G           Am          C
And the weather is hot, and the weather is cold,
                F                          G7
And there are storms from a cyclone to behold.
             C         G        Am    C
There's dense fog cover everywhere -
        F                           G7
Great floods somewhere else, so I don't care.

            C     C*           F          Am     G7
God will save us - let's hope that He exists,
                C     C*          F         Am     G7
As we are on a foreign ferry with a nasty list.

                    **********

           C   G           Am    C
We are on a boat; we are on a plane;
           F                  G7
We are on a bus, and we can't complain.
           C   G         Am   C
We are on a bike; we are in a car;
           F            G7
We are walking, as it's not too far.

     C   C*F          Am     G7
We speculate on the Bible code,
              C     C*        F          Am     G7
As the bombs from the terrorists do explode.
```

****

```
     C        G              Am       C
We buy computers and we buy new chairs;
   F              G7
We buy shampoo to wash our hairs.
   C        G            Am       C
We buy new cars and houses too;
   F              G7
We visit the park and visit the zoo.
           C    C*     F         Am        G7
Let's sing out of Spring and Summer now;
      C    C*       F        Am        G7
Get Autumn and Winter in there somehow.
```

****

```
        C              G      Am          C
Now bring all those carbon footprints down;
 F           G7
Ecology has come to town.
          C           G      Am       C
Let's tackle youth culture in the schools,
   F           G7
So obesity no longer rules.
            C              C*         F    Am   G7
Who'd have thought that nice young chap next door
              C       C*    F      Am    G7
Could have murdered forty people, maybe more.
```

****

```
       C        G     Am        C
It's Easter and it's just the same
   F              G7
For any festival you care to name.
      C       G         Am     C
It's Christmas time, let's all be merry;
          F                  G7
Throw up over the side of a cross channel ferry.

      C       G         Am     C
It's Christmas time, let's all be merry;
          F                  G7
Throw up over the side of a cross channel ferry.

      C       G         Am     C
It's Christmas time, let's all be merry;
          F                  G7                  C
Throw up over the side of a cross channel ferry.
```

~*~*~*~*~

The Creative Arts

'Hello Rufus, how's my favourite broadsheet art critic?'

'I'm very well thanks, Max. How are you?'

'Flourishing. What are you up to at the moment?'

'I'm on the panel of judges for the National Poetry Competition. We've been working on the shortlist this morning, although it will be one of the usual contenders that gets it.'

'How can you be so sure? Aren't the identities of the writers kept secret from the judges until you've selected the best work?'

'God no, Max! That would lead to complete chaos.'

'Why?'

'Well, there's no way of telling, just by reading it, whether a poem has been written by one of the greatest contemporary British poets or by a dyslexic fourth former from Neasden Comprehensive. If we awarded prizes to other than credible, established poets, the whole literary edifice would collapse.'

'In that case, Rufus, how *do* you choose the winner?'

'It doesn't matter. We usually drop all the shortlisted entries in the toilet and then flush it. Usually one doesn't go down the pan properly, so we fish it out and declare that poet the winner. It's the shortlist that's critical.'

'In what way?'

'Well, Max, shortlisted writers must be publicly recognised as poets and be able to talk knowledgeably about poetry and literature and about those who have been their literary influences. If someone can convincingly expound the right pseudo-intellectual bullshit, it will be accepted that his or her writing must be suitably profound to be, somehow, special and different. As long as such a person wins, then the credibility of the art-form is maintained.'

'Is that also true for the rest of the Arts, Rufus?'

'Mostly. Take photography: These days there's no knowledge required to take a technically good photograph. Any spotty kid with a camera on his mobile phone will regularly take pictures that are indistinguishable from those of leading creative photographers. If that fact got out, it would never again be possible to hold fashionable photographic exhibitions or launch stylish photo-websites.'

'I must admit I *had* wondered about the Turner Prize.'

'A very good example of the same thing, Max.'

'Why should we be conned into believing in a fantasy world? Shouldn't this deception be exposed?'

'Too dangerous, Max.'

'Why?'

'Because Art reflects Life, Max. People use it as a way to understand the world. If people saw through the Art Delusion, where would it all end?'

'I don't understand.'

'We saw in the stock market crashes after 9/11, Max, how financial stability is based on investor confidence. Just think of the consequences if people really understood that the money in their pockets was only real for as long as they believed it was real? What would happen if religious beliefs were seen as a convenient collective understanding rather than as objective fact? There would be financial and moral meltdown.'

'So, Rufus, if the creative arts are ever seen as meaningless self-indulgent fantasy, people might start to recognise other critical institutions in that way too. That could lead to the end of civilisation as we know it!'

'Absolutely right, my old friend. Now, I've got the shortlisted entries for the National Poetry Competition in my briefcase. Do you know the way to the nearest lavatory?'

~*~*~*~

Neighbours

For very many years, my wife and I have been passionate devotees of soap operas. *Coronation Street, Crossroads, Neighbours, Emmerdale, Home and Away, Hollyoaks, Doctors, Eastenders* and, of course, *The Archers* on the radio - we have rarely missed any episode. In recent times, however, storylines have seemed less compelling and series have lost their engaging spark.

Initially, this seemed unrelated to the sad death of our elderly next-door neighbour and the arrival of a family in what had been his adjoining semi-detached house. The wall connecting our properties is thin, however, and loud verbal manifestations of their marital discord soon became a daily occurrence.

At first, this was somewhat irritating. Their clarity of diction and the volume of their voices, however, were such that we began to listen to the fascinating content. Indeed, we became disappointed when their speech resumed normal levels and became more difficult to hear.

I teach acoustics and audio electronics so it was simple to strategically connect microphones to our connecting wall and render all next-door's conversations with perfect fidelity. It was better than any soap. Among our new neighbours, their family and friends were real-life storylines of which soap writers could only dream: marital discord, infidelity, alcohol and drug abuse, criminality, sexual misbehaviour, truancy, juvenile crime, teenage pregnancy and so on. It was all there! We abandoned pale, fictional substitutes and listened to little else.

However, George and Lynn, who live across the road, soon detected something unusual. They too were devoted followers of the soaps and noticed very quickly that we were no longer up to date with current plots. We had to confess our new, alternative listening habits. Soon they were joining us each evening to keep up with developments at number twenty-four.

As word reached other friends, however, our front room became uncomfortably overcrowded. Also, as the most interesting dialogue occurred at random times throughout the day, everyone complained about missing critical twists in the plot. I therefore began to make recordings, edit these into half-hour programmes and make them accessible on a password-protected Internet site.

All was well until we noticed that one of our friends, Henry, was starting an affair with the wife of the couple. When confronted, he admitted that he had always wanted to be in a soap opera and had seen this as his chance. We thus formed an editorial committee to approve any deliberate interventions into the plot. This has proven very useful during the inevitable quiet and unexciting periods in the lives of our neighbours. Examples include the theft of their car, the burglary, and the affair of the husband with Joyce from Station Drive. We vetoed the house fire and flooding suggestions, firstly on grounds that we were living in the connected semi, but also that evacuation or destruction of their property would end the current source of recordings.

We have now developed a year long archive of daily episodes, and have begun to ponder their commercial value. Clearly, it would be difficult to broadcast these in the UK on a channel to which our neighbours might listen. We have, however, had some signs of interest from the States…

~*~*~*~*~

The Sport

Early in the twenty-first century, the British Government had begun to greatly encourage sport. It soon became apparent, however, that allocating resources to hundreds of different sporting organisations was highly inefficient. This led the Minister for Miscellaneous Loose Ends, who maintained responsibility for such matters, to return to fundamentals. What, he asked, was the purpose of sport?

On that point, there was universal agreement: The purpose of sport was to raise revenue through advertising and merchandising. It followed, therefore, that there was little point in having a multitude of unrelated sports: All should be combined to form a single, all-embracing entity – The Sport.

This concept was enthusiastically accepted. The Devil, however, was in the detail. Despite the inception of The Sport some thirty years ago, the International Sport Rules Formulation Committee has yet to complete its work. Should the offside rule apply, for example, if a player is holding a snooker cue while standing in the crease? How would that be modified if he or she were underwater and/or on horseback at the time? Similar problems have dogged the International Sport Pitch Specification Committee: How could it be possible, they have argued, to accommodate, on a relatively small table, up to twenty-seven players and a kangaroo?

All this was resolved, or at least made academic, by the International Sport Referees Committee. They concluded that, even if the rules and venue issues could be resolved, The Sport could never be played: The elements derived from cricket would lead to cancellation in rain or bad light; those derived from skiing could not accommodate high temperatures; those related to swimming could not cope with very low temperatures; those having their basis in English football would be called off due to mindless crowd violence, and so on. When the characteristics of all constituent sports were considered, there were no conditions in which The Sport would not be cancelled before it began.

For those of us who are international Sport superstars, this revelation came as something of a relief. Years of uncertainty about the rules, together with no practice or training, had made us very anxious about the prospect of being called upon to take to the field, track, pitch, pool, course, table or whatever.

Also, of course, where would we have found the time? As one of the world's leading Sport stars, I have lucrative sponsorship deals with manufactures of watches, toiletry products, electronics, alcohol, crisps and fast food - also supermarket chains, fashion houses and record companies. My time is totally devoted to photo-shoots and product launches.

Many of my fellow superstars have entered the world of publishing. Inspired by the autobiography of Wayne Rooney, published in 2006, some recently conceived fertilised embryos in the pre-foetal stage have risen to Sport stardom and had their life stories, so far, ghost written in three hundred pages of unusually large script.

I, however, will shortly be retiring. Sales of Sport shirts with my name on the back, and my famous number, 786451462789.75, seem to have limitless sales potential in China. This revenue alone should keep me in comfort for the rest of my days. The Sport is definitely 'The Beautiful Game'.

~*~*~*~*~

A Few Words from Marcus

Here at Dog Rescue we try our utmost to re-home the animals that come into our care. Sometimes, this is easy. Puppies and older, well-trained family pets are in great demand. Sadly, some of our less popular canines remain with us for very many months.

In order to encourage visitors to consider our longer-standing residents, it is my job to write some inspiring words about them to attach to their enclosures. I write such notes as if from the perspectives of the creatures themselves. This can warm the hearts of potential owners, and I know that my writings have been an important initial factor in many successful rehomings.

Marcus was my greatest challenge. But let me tell you his story in his own words - as written by me.

'Hello, my name is Marcus. You might think I look rather large and fierce. That is because my daddy was a Rottweiler and my mummy was a Doberman/Pit Bull cross. I had a happy puppyhood, living wild with my parents in woodland near Bodmin. What fun we had hunting rabbits and other creatures such as cats, dogs, sheep and small children.

Unfortunately, bigger people were not very kind to us. They kept trying to shoot us, and eventually they succeeded in killing my mummy and daddy, leaving me an orphan. I was forced to move onto the Moor and fend for myself with little to eat but sheep, cattle and hikers.

Eventually I was caught by the army and placed with the nice people at Dog Rescue. I am really looking forward to finding a new home. Because I can sometimes be a little bad tempered and don't really like people, the Home Office prefer me to wear a muzzle and live in a carbon fibre reinforced steel cage. Nevertheless, I would be an ideal pet for a patient and caring owner with experience in treating rabies.'

The usual applicants for a dog such as Marcus soon came forward. There was the single mother with three small children, and one on the way, who thought a large, untrained dog would be an ideal addition to the family. Then there was the middle-aged lady living alone and on benefits on the fourteenth floor of a council tower block, who had already taken in twenty-five stray dogs and forty cats. Finally there was the short, overweight, tattooed, macho, unemployed and not very bright labourer who was seeking a dog to match his self-image. As usual, we had to advise them all against re-homing.

One day, however, the canine psychologist from the TV show 'Dogs from Hell' arrived looking for a subject for his next programme. Marcus was ideal. In no time the Marcus of old could hardly be recognised, covered, as he was, in human blood and smashed TV recording equipment.

He was last seen heading back to his home on Bodmin Moor, where he has now become something of a legend.

~*~*~*~

The Actress

I had dreamed of becoming an actress
Since playing in many a scene
At school and in amateur drama.
I longed for the cinema screen.

So I strove to attend drama college
And passed all exams from the start.
I graduated with distinction
Then started to search for a part.

Imagine my joy when my agent
Found my very first role on TV:
In *Morse* with the spires of Oxford -
In the opening scene I would be.

My joy turned to some disappointment
When I learned I would not make a sound,
But simply float face down in water
In the Thames - as a victim who drowned.

That role, though, then led to another:
In *The Bill* – yet another cop show:
My foot now appeared in a mortuary scene
With a label tied round my big toe.

I worried about being typecast,
But the payments I could not forego
As the corpse in the library Miss Marple would find
Or a body exhumed by Poirot.

I finally spoke to my agent:
'You must find a new genre,' I said.
'I will never break into the Hollywood scene
If I only play people who're dead.'

He found a new part, though not speaking
In an advert to be on TV
To promote the effects of a haemorrhoid cream -
Portraying relief would be me!

Regretfully, similar followed:
Diarrhoea, a thrush remedy,
Constipation, verrucas and unwanted hair,
Gonorrhoea then warts and acne.

Once I had dreamed of the public
Recognising my face in the street.
Now I dreaded the eagle-eyed fan who would say:
'You're the one with the clap and bad feet!'

It was then that repeats of the cop shows
Brought a regular income from fees.
And the wart ad - it took off in China
Producing its own royalties.

I'd just earned enough to retire
When a script arrived for me to see.
My agent said it was the part of a lifetime
That could have been written for me.

The heroine's many conditions
I'd portrayed in my advert heyday,
And right at the start of the opening scene
She keeled over - and then passed away.

My career, it had led to that moment.
It was also my first speaking part:
Just prior to tumbling down to the ground
I screamed 'Ahh' and then clutched at my heart.

I regret now my lack of an Oscar,
But a great consolation to me
Is that death and unsocial diseases
Were portrayed with extreme quality.

I live now in Spain in a villa.
An actress,' I say, when enquired.
If asked of the parts I have played, I reply:
'I don't talk of that, now – I'm retired.'

~*~*~*~*~

The Shop

I glanced at the summit of Ben Nevis, three hundred feet above. There was, sadly, no path. I had deviated from the main track and trekked some distance along the wrong gully. I was about to retrace my steps when I came upon an incongruous, glazed, aluminium door in the cliff. It slid open on my approach. I stepped through.

Before me lay a vast cavern, housing row upon row of laden shelves. I proceeded in amazement along a grocery-lined aisle, pausing at instant coffee. Briefly forgetting my bewilderment, I picked up a jar and glanced at the price - some four times more expensive than I usually paid.

'Hello,' said a voice behind me.

I turned in surprise to see a middle aged man in a supermarket uniform with the name 'George' on his lapel badge.

'Would you like to buy some coffee?' George enquired.

'It's a bit expensive,' I pointed out.

'Absurdly so,' he concurred.

I replaced the jar. 'What is this place?'

'It's a shop,' said George, surprised at having to state the obvious. 'It's got the largest range of stock in the UK – everything from coffee to cars.'

'I imagine you don't get many customers?'

'Just the occasional lost walker,' George confirmed. 'And no one buys anything at these prices.'

'Then what's the point?' I gestured around me.

'Special offers,' George explained. 'Before any UK product can be sold at a discounted price, it must be on sale for a month at the original, higher price. One item of each product is put on sale here for that month.' He paused for thought. 'Would you like a cup of tea?'

'How much?' I cautiously queried.

'Free.'

George led the way past garden equipment, electrical goods and fashion, around building materials and through the car showroom to where some chairs and tables stood beside a row of kiosks.

I sat down as my guide poured tea. The sign on the nearest kiosk read 'North Korean Government Complaints Department'.

George anticipated my question: 'The shop serves other functions. For example, all North Koreans who wish to complain about their government must do so here, in person.'

'Do many come?' I queried.

'Not so far – some problem with exit visas. British Government departments are represented here too.' He gestured towards another kiosk. 'People who wish to appeal against refusal of disability benefits have to present their cases at that counter.'

'How do they expect a disabled person to reach a concealed cave near the top of Ben Nevis?'

'Exactly!' he continued as he gave me my tea. 'That's the clever bit. Any cases presented here are proven bogus!' He sat down. 'All asylum claims must now be lodged here too.'

'Where's the counter for asylum seekers?' I said, looking around me.

'I'm not sure,' George admitted. 'I've never been there. It's somewhere much deeper inside the mountain. I believe it's down a pothole and beyond several freezing, water filled sumps.'

I consulted my watch. 'Thanks for the tea,' I said, 'but I must go or I won't reach the summit and complete my descent before nightfall.'

As I rejoined the main track, visibility was decreasing. I had already lost sight of the doorway, and, as I glanced back, its gully was also vanishing, Shangri-la-like, into the mist.

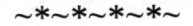

~*~*~*~*~

Expo Riva Schuh

Inspector Limone sipped an aperol spritz and looked across the Piazza 3 Novembre to the entrance of the Hotel Sole. In the absence of a Hotel Upper in Riva del Garda, this was the accommodation of choice for delegates attending the International Shoe Fair, Expo Riva Schuh.

The Fair was always a potential flashpoint as highly strung footwear designers vied for fashion prominence. Last year, four exhibitors from Calabria, the toe of Italy, had been assassinated by a delegate from the region of Puglia, Italy's heel. The perpetrator had used bootleg Grappa, laced with poison.

Limone had been assigned to ensure that, this year, all toed the line.

Reliable intelligence indicated that there were plans afoot for Luigi Slingbacci to eliminate his arch rival in the high heel eveningwear category, Giuseppe Pumpello. It was known that Luigi would take this step today, but not when or how.

Limone saw Giuseppe leave the hotel and wondered if his cane concealed a knife. The risks of the Fair were such that most participants employed some form of self protection. Luigi followed just a few yards behind, guarded by his young Rottweiler, Etto.

Limone rose and jogged hotfoot in pursuit across the Piazza Catena where he followed the men onto a ferry. The required turn of speed winded him, and he reflected on the need for a personal trainer, maybe even a pair.

Luigi sat down on the foredeck, directly behind Giuseppe. Although Limone recognised both men from photographs, he had never met either and so was able to take a seat unnoticed next to Luigi and his dog.

The Rottweiler growled at Limone. 'Still, Etto. Heel!' commanded Luigi in a strong regional brogue.

That brogue was a fine shoe, Limone noted to himself as Luigi put on the other.

A stiff breeze blew across Lake Garda, building waves that caused the Verona to toss and roll during the crossing, and even as the boat docked at Torbole.

Giuseppe and Luigi remained seated as other passengers disembarked. Suddenly, Limone noted a puff of dust kicked up from the deck in front of Luigi's right shoe. He realised immediately that the brogue concealed a dart gun. This was a shoe-ting!

At that exact moment, the ferry pitched with the impact of another wave. The dart missed the back of Giuseppe's leg, ricocheted from the iron boat side and struck Etto, who was at once a hushed puppy.

Limone lept to his feet, drew his gun and levelled it at Luigi. 'Remove your shoes,' he ordered.

'It's a shoe-jacking!' shouted frightened witnesses, familiar with this phenomenon from the time of the last Expo Riva Schuh. Panicking passengers left their shoes and fled barefoot down the gangway onto the quay.

Before departing with his prisoner, Limone stood atop the gangway and quickly composed a farewell speech to the crowd on the quayside. He explained the true nature of his actions, police determination to defeat pedal criminality and the legal right of those present to reclaim their footwear.

Four days of the Fair remained. Limone knew there would be other incidents. Today, however, he was gratified that he had 'snatched victory from the jaws of defeat', and, when addressing the crowd, had also 'hatched a valedictory from the laws of the feet'.

~*~*~*~

7 – Politics and the Law

Change You Can Believe In

The newly elected British Prime Minister gazed from a Downing Street window at the gigantic, yellow plastic duck that towered above all London's buildings.

He recalled a time when politicians had ideologies to promote and cared passionately about issues of the day. Gradual changes of attitude had occurred until the expenses scandal of 2009 awakened the public realisation that politicians had become amoral and self-serving.

Political statements had become simply contrived arguments aimed at attributing any negative event to a rival. Without a moral or ideological compass, personal gain had become the primary objective of British politicians.

Voter frustration and cynicism drove election turn-outs to the lowest ever recorded.

It was in this climate, and on the eve of a mid-term parliamentary election, that three factors contributed to Nigel Smith, the Liberal Democrat candidate for Snodbury West, changing the course of British politics.

The first was his reading of a Monster Raving Loony Party manifesto. The second was certainty that he had no prospect of becoming elected. Finally, he was distraught when he learned of his wife's affairs with both the Labour and Conservative candidates.

Despite these influences, Nigel was never totally sure what had driven him to commit his party, in a television interview, to providing, if elected, a lifetime supply of free custard to all Snodbury residents.

Next day, the local Party and the national leadership faced a political dilemma. Should they condemn Nigel for making stupid statements that brought the Party into disrepute, or should he be applauded on his election to Parliament with one hundred percent of the Snodbury West vote on a one hundred percent voter turnout?

There quickly followed another mid-term election for the London Borough of Westford, and again the Liberal Democrats had no expectations of victory. Emboldened by Nigel's surrealist success, however, the candidate championed the removal of all the Borough's road signs.

This second landslide victory confirmed the mood of the British public. All interest had been lost in traditional politics, but the British sense of comic irony remained, and votes could be guaranteed for the most silly manifesto pledge.

As the General Election approached, amorality and self-interest made it easy for parliamentary candidates to cease campaigning on social, economic and security issues in favour of increasingly bizarre and pointless follies.

Labour's plan to paint all grass pink proved popular, as did the Conservative proposal to build a ladder to the moon - it was going to be a close run contest. Then Nigel formulated his masterstroke of political and comic genius – the Liberal Democrats would honour their manifesto commitments!

Convoys of custard tankers arrived in Snodbury. Traffic ground to a halt in Westford.

Other parties argued it unfair and contrary to parliamentary tradition to take seriously promises to the electorate, but public support was won. The Liberal Democrat election slogan, 'Insane Ideas, Implemented!!!', was something in which the people could finally believe.

Even the closure of schools and hospitals by the former government to fund The London Duck could not save them from defeat.

Nigel Smith, Britain's first Liberal Democrat Prime Minister, turned from the window of Number Ten and donned two large ears and a tail to complete his kangaroo costume. Politics had indeed changed, he reflected as he hopped to the door and into the street where the media awaited the delivery of his inaugural stand-up routine to the Nation.

~*~*~*~*~

Promotin' Effective Parentin'

I'd never bin able to control me kids. They'd just done what they liked an' kept gettin' into trouble.

Then, about three years back, I got a visit from the Council. They said the Government 'ad decided to solve the problem of young people's anti-social behaviour once an' for all. They was goin' to take their parents to court, an' maybe send us to prison.

At first I thought this was a stupid idea thought up by some ignorant, right wing, middle class twit of a politician who 'ad no concept of the complex inter-relationships between social deprivation, education an' anti-social behaviour. Either it was the first thought they'd ever 'ad on the subject or the first thought they believed might get 'em votes from other ignorant, right wing, middle class twits who 'ad no concept of the complex inter-relationships between social deprivation, education an' anti-social behaviour.

'Ow wrong I was. I ended up in prison, sure enough, but it was the best thing that ever 'appened for me an' me kids. From the day I was released, the kids 'ave never bin in trouble again.

When I got out, I gave me eldest, Tom, a good talkin' to. In prison, I'd spend a lot of time with Fingers McNab from cell twenty-three. 'E'd explained the best way to break into 'ouses; which areas to target; 'ow to plan the location an' timin' of break-ins to fool the police; an' 'ow to safely fence the nicked stuff. Fingers was caught when 'e was grassed-up by a mate. 'E reckoned if 'e'd worked alone an' never said nothin' to no one, 'e'd 'ave got away with it.

Tom's a bright lad, an' 'e's made a fortune usin' Fingers' methods, without the Bill ever 'avin' a clue.

I next spoke to me lad, George. 'E's always bin keen on gardenin' an' so really took to the tips about growin' cannabis that Leroy from cell thirty-five 'ad passed on to me. Leroy was caught 'cos 'e got greedy. 'E reckoned 'e should 'ave stopped when 'e'd made a million.

George reached that target six months ago an' shut down 'is cannabis factory in the attic.

'Enry, me youngest, is great on the computer, so 'e really liked the Internet scams that got Pete from cell fifty-four nicked. Pete said 'e should have covered 'is tracks better, so 'Enry worked from me van usin' different unencrypted wireless networks. 'E then used software to keep 'is 'ard drive bleached. Finally, 'e followed Leroy's Golden Rule of not gettin' greedy, an' quit when 'e'd made two million.

Me, I've always bin into cars, an', with the advice and contacts I got from John in cell eighty-one, I made nearly a million from nickin' an' sellin'-on high value, top-end motors.

Well, 'ere we all are in our new villa on Spain's Costa Tropical. We're all gonna take a break for a few months an' then start up a couple of legit businesses to keep our new lifestyle tickin' over.

As I sit 'ere by the pool, drinkin' Cava, I only wish I could thank whoever it was that suggested imprisonin' deprived and disadvantaged parents with poor parentin' skills as a way of stoppin' their kids gettin' arrested. It was a stroke of fuckin' genius.

~*~*~*~*~

Guiltman

I inspected the setting concrete that was transforming my front garden into a parking area. Just a six foot by three foot section remained to pour.

Suddenly, my attention was drawn to an object flying high in the sky, but descending rapidly towards me. Was it a bird? Was it a plane? In an instant a masked, caped and leotard clad figure landed by my side.

'Who are you?' I said, noting the imposing letter G emblazoned upon his chest.

'I am Guiltman,' announced the figure. 'I am a superhero. I have come to make you feel guilty about concreting your front garden.'

I was puzzled. 'Why?'

'Because it will compromise drainage and contribute to flooding risk.'

'Shouldn't you be deflecting asteroids or foiling supervillains?' I responded with irritation.

'That's a bit twentieth century,' he replied disparagingly. 'These days we superheroes target ordinary people who are driving the planet to ecological ruin or eschewing healthy lifestyles.' He pointed his finger accusingly at me. 'People like you!' he emphasised in a decisive and judgmental tone.

I picked up my spade and began to deepen the trench for the final concrete pour. 'Is there anything else I should be feeling guilty about?' I enquired.

'It's a long list,' he answered. 'Your house isn't adequately insulated; your television is mostly left on standby; you don't use energy saving lightbulbs; you rarely buy organic produce; you don't usually buy Fairtrade products; you buy products with excessive packaging; your car has an unnecessarily large engine; you drive when you could walk; you don't take enough exercise; you're overweight; you eat too much fat, sugar and salt; you rarely have five portions of vegetables a day; you drink more than twenty-one units of alcohol per week – sometimes per day; you smoke; you take holidays with high carbon footprints; you rarely recycle; you don't compost…'

By the time his list was complete I had finished digging. 'Many of those things could be said about most people,' I observed, 'and some are what make life fun.'

'If it's fun,' replied Guiltman, 'it's almost certainly unhealthy or ecologically unsound – that's one way you can tell! If you're enjoying yourself, you should always stop and feel particularly guilty.'

I climbed from my excavation. 'You've now told me everything I should feel guilty about. What happens next?'

Guiltman turned away from me and looked skyward. 'I must journey onwards,' he pronounced with a majestic and heroic voice. 'Each house in this road, each road in this town and each town in this land must be visited to maximise the burden of twenty-first century worry and guilt assailing every citizen!'

'You've certainly convinced me that I should do my bit for mankind,' I conceded, as my spade connected with the back of his head.

Guiltman slumped forwards into the hole, and I was gratified that I had correctly estimated the extra depth required to accommodate the body.

It was early evening as I levelled the final section of concrete. It had been a hard day's work, but my new *Ferrari* would be arriving in a day or two, so the parking area had to be finished. Now I would drive to get a takeaway and a wine box for the evening. Then I could relax without a care in the world.

~*~*~*~*~

Alarm at Increase in Crimes for Charity

Public outcry has followed release of new government figures showing a large increase in crimes committed for charity.

The growth of this phenomenon has been linked with the end of the TV appeals, *Comic Relief* and *Children in Need*.

Initially, significant revenue was generated from these events as fundraisers undertook numerous humiliating and pointless activities. When the novelty wore off, however, charity activists and media personalities were much less inclined to place themselves in cringingly embarrassing situations which would perennially come back to haunt them.

Also the public became increasingly unwilling to pretend to be entertained by such behaviours. Indeed, in the final year of the above appeals, donors overwhelmingly sponsored individuals not to undertake their threatened acts of self degradation.

Unfortunately, the end of such appeals precipitated a revenue crisis, forcing charity activists to seek other ways of raising much needed funds for humanitarian appeals.

Tragically, more and more charities turned to crime.

Fitzgerald Y, a stockbroker from Mayfair, was attacked near his home. 'They've no right to do this,' he told police. 'They said my Rolex was going to pay for after school clubs for kids on council estates. If I hadn't been mugged, I certainly wouldn't have given anything to that sort of undeserving rabble.'

No stratum of society has been spared. Leroy X, a South London drug dealer, was returning home with several thousand pounds after a successful day of dealing when four smartly dressed men with middle class accents approached him. 'They grabbed me an' said I was bein' mugged for charity,' he angrily told reporters. 'They said me cash would be payin' for wells in f****n' Africa.'

Charity burglaries have also increased, with televisions, media players and computers either being fenced for funds to help Third World projects, or being shipped directly to those in need.

There is evidence that this is an international problem. Blackmail is suspected to be behind the timely provision of tents and emergency supplies to relieve the humanitarian crisis in North Africa. 'We became suspicious when aid arrangements were put in place in good time to address a long predicted famine,' said an Interpol spokesman. 'The official international response has characteristically been "too little: too late", so we immediately knew something was wrong.'

The politicians and captains of industry who made substantial personal donations to avert the disaster denied that they had been victims of blackmail. 'I was going to give the money anyway...oops,' said one senior European leader.

Church leaders have condemned events such as *Mugging-Aid*, *Burgling-Aid* and *Armed-Building-Society-Robbery-Aid*. It is believed, however, that profits from such activities have funded a number of church roof, spire and tower repairs via the seemingly innocuous *Fell-Off-The-Back-Of-A-Lorry-Aid* and *Bought-From-A-Man-Down-The-Pub-Aid*.

It is even reported that traditional criminal organisations are concerned about the infiltration of undercover charity workers into their ranks. 'We are aware that funds earmarked for contract killings have been diverted to housing projects for the poor in Naples,' confessed a Mafia spokes-hit-person.

Official advice to members of the public is to remain calm. If approached by someone with a charity collecting box, however, the safest option remains to hand over wallets or handbags to avoid the risk of escalating violence.

~*~*~*~

He Seemed So Ordinary

'Hello, this is the Crimestoppers' telephone helpline. How can I assist you?'

'I think the police should know about my neighbour.'

'In what way?'

'I think he might be a rapist or serial killer or terrorist or something like that.'

'What's made you suspicious?'

'He just seems so ordinary. I don't know him very well, but he appears to be very nice. He always says a friendly 'hello' when I meet him in the street. You wouldn't think there was anything odd about him at all. He's the very last person you'd suspect of any wrongdoing.'

'I agree that sounds a bit worrying. I'm glad you contacted us. This kind of neighbour description has been typical of some of our most dangerous and notorious criminals. What else do you know about him?'

'I see his wife sometimes. She seems pleasant enough. I think she helps out at the local school. Do you think she might be involved?'

'It's hard to say. She'll probably never be prosecuted, but we'll all suspect that she must have known something. After all, those heinous crimes would have taken place right under her nose and over a long period.'

'I think they're both involved in charity work.'

'That's a bad sign. It's a classic strategy to select victims whilst allaying suspicion. He's not involved with the Church, is he?'

'Yes, he preaches at St Michael's.'

'Oh God! This sounds even more serious than I first feared.'

'Why?'

'Those who minister in the Church tend to have their crimes go undetected for much longer periods. It's quite likely that he's been abusing vulnerable members of his congregation for years in addition to his other catalogue of terrifying and horrific offences.'

'What are you going to do?'

'I think the police will want to act quickly. What you've told me already sounds pretty conclusive. What's his name and address?'

'Henry Smith of 14, Acacia Drive.'

'That's a frighteningly nondescript name and address – once again typical of this kind of monster. He drives a white Mondeo, doesn't he?'

'How did you know?'

'Have you ever known a criminal in a Crimewatch reconstruction drive anything else?'

'Now you come to mention it…'

'Of course, all the offences he will have committed thirty years ago - the worrying crimes which would have clearly linked him to recent sickening and depraved acts - will have gone unnoticed by police enquiries.'

'What will have gone wrong?'

'Typically, in cases like this, there will have been a simple error by the police that will have led them to overlook key evidence and hence not make the vital connections. I expect the Chief Constable will have to resign again.

'What shall I do now?'

'Nothing. The police will pick him up today and release him due to lack of evidence. He will commit one more crime and then be arrested, tried in a blaze of publicity and finally imprisoned. Don't worry though, you'll be perfectly safe. They never harm the neighbours. In fact, you're the first neighbour who's ever suspected anything.'

~*~*~*~*~

The Consultation Period

Luigi backed towards the wall, his hands above his head. He looked down the black barrel of the handgun that was being levelled at him by a smartly dressed stranger.

'Is this a contact hit?' Luigi asked.

'Yes,' replied the stranger, 'you seem to have offended the Sicilian Mafia. They've put one hundred thousand dollars on your head, and that money's got my name on it.' The stranger gestured with the gun towards a chair. 'Sit down.'

'What's the point? Why don't you just shoot?'

'Can't just shoot you,' the gunman explained: 'I'll have to await the outcome of the consultation process.'

'Consultation process?'

'Yes.' The stranger withdrew some papers from his pocket and passed then to Luigi. 'Those documents explain options in relation to the proposal to shoot you, and they give you an opportunity to make any comments and suggestions before final decisions are made.'

Luigi ventured his opinion. 'I don't want to be shot.'

'I believe that's one of the options, although you will need to complete the consultation form and return it to me.'

'How long's the consultation period?'

'The standard five minutes.'

Luigi inspected the documents. 'If I write that I prefer the 'not being shot' option, will you let me go?'

'I can't really comment on the outcome of the consultation process until all submissions have been received.'

'How many submissions will there be?'

'Including yours, one. I should get writing if I were you, you're getting close to the consultation deadline.'

Luigi wrote on the form that he preferred the 'not being shot' option, and quickly passed the papers back to the stranger. 'You've already decided you're going to shoot, haven't you?' he said, angrily. 'This consultation process is just a sham.'

'I can assure you,' the assassin responded, 'that your views will be very carefully considered and fully taken into account. I would also like to thank you for taking the time to participate in the debate on this important local issue.'

Luigi's potential assailant lifted his dark glasses and peered thoughtfully at the consultation paperwork. 'There are clearly differences of viewpoint,' he noted, 'between those favouring the 'not being shot' option and those supporting the 'preferred strategy'.'

'What's the 'preferred strategy?''

'That's where I shoot you and collect the money.'

'Who decides on the 'preferred strategy?''

'There's always a 'preferred strategy'. That's what those with the power have already decided is going to happen.'

'So the consultation process is a sham!'

'Not at all. It gives people an opportunity to express their viewpoints, make suggestions and proposals, and democratically participate in the decision making process. No consultation process has ever claimed that anyone who mattered gave a shit about those comments – even less that they might act on them.'

The tone of the hit-man changed to one of polite formality. 'Many thanks to all those who contributed to the consultation process on the proposed assassination of Luigi Napoli. The views expressed have very much informed the thinking on this matter. I am now please to be in a position to let you know the outcome.'

BANG.

~*~*~*~*~

Santa's Reindeer

It was Christmas Eve on the High Street,
The vendors were dressed for a laugh -
With checkout girls sporting red Santa hats,
And elf helpers for post office staff.

Outside the Bank a van screeched to a halt,
Eight raiders rushed in at a canter.
I was heartened they too joined the seasonal fun,
Wearing masks of the reindeer of Santa.

Alarm bells contributed festival sounds,
Gunshots could have fireworks been,
As the reindeer effected a hasty retreat,
Pursued by an armed response team.

It was clear the Police had known of the raid,
A matter which made me quite restive,
As they simply had worn their black, bullet-proof vests,
And made no attempt to be festive.

Dasher spun round and attempted to fire,
A move which I thought quite unwise.
The first police shot blew an antler away,
The second was right 'twixt the eyes.

One six year old spoke for the child of today -
Innocence, street wisdom laced:
'Santa will be very cross with his deer -
Least the ones that the Filth do not waste.'

Dancer and Prancer and Vixen
Reached the Shopping Mall's Christmas display,
Whilst Comet and Cupid and Donner and Blitzen
Were abruptly gunned down on the way.

With toy elves, a sleigh and some snowmen
Stood a real, living Santa that morning.
'Get back or the fat, bearded guy is dead meat.'
Prancer shouted his desperate warning.

The children, they scattered in terror,
Then confided their one greatest fear:
'If that naughty old reindeer kills Santa,
Will we get any presents this year?'

It was lucky that this stand-in Santa
Had a plan to escape from the mess,
As he liked to play Santa by way of a break
From instructing for the SAS.

A deft move left Prancer's neck broken,
Then he grabbed for the gun and spun round.
Two perfect aimed gunshots with lightening speed
Sent the other two deer to the ground.

The teenagers out with their parents
Would disparage this scene as a rule,
But were forced to revise their opinions
And reclassify Santa as 'cool'.

The Police and our Santa, they counted
The venison there laying dead.
'We've got eight but, shit, there's one missing.
Where the bugger is Rudolf?' they said.

They quickly glanced back down the High Street.
The vehicle still by the bank lay.
'He's the driver', they suddenly realised,
As the getaway van sped away.

It raced off at full speed towards them,
The Police and our Santa fired lead.
The van hit a tree and exploded,
The last robber-reindeer was dead.

Two pensioners spoke in a doorway:
'Now somehow it seems to me, dear,
That Christmas, as well as expensive,
Is rather more violent, this year.'

~*~*~*~*~

All UK Crime Solved!

The British Police lead the world in catching criminals – and that's official! British Government statistics, published this week, show that there are no outstanding unsolved crimes in the UK. This contrasts dramatically with the picture just twelve months ago when there had been no successful convictions in UK courts for nearly two years.

This remarkable achievement is credited to Commander Ernest Booker who was controversially appointed to head of the British Police last year from his previous role as a trainee junior traffic officer. Commander Booker had been undertaking a remedial course in basic numeracy when he had experienced his brilliant inspiration. He already knew that UK crime statistics could only be improved by a seemingly impossible increase in the number of successful convictions. His work as a traffic officer, however, led him to realise that this was possible in relation to one category of offences – parking violations.

He reasoned that if just one crime was committed in a period, for example a murder, with no subsequent conviction, then the statistics would show one hundred percent of crimes as being unsolved. If nine hundred and ninety-nine parking violators were apprehended in the same period, however, the murderer at large would have simply amended the unsolved crime statistics to one in a thousand, or zero point zero-zero-one percent. Even the activities of a prolific serial killer would still represent just a small fraction of one percent of total crime. With large enough numbers of convicted parking violators, the percentage of unsolved crimes could be made statistically insignificant and be considered as zero.

Immediately following his appointment, Commander Booker had reassigned all police officers from non-essential bodies such as murder squads, rape investigation teams and anti-terrorist units, to undertake parking violation enforcement. He also applied discretionary police powers to introduce the offence of 'stopping or parking a vehicle anywhere, at any time'.

Tickets were issued to stationary vehicles in their hundreds of thousands. Halting at traffic lights, stopping for fuel at petrol stations or parking in ones own garage were considered as no defence. Police cars would tail normally law-abiding motorists for miles on suspicion of 'intent to stop' and serve ticket after ticket for each failure to maintain forward momentum. Corporate owners of automotive production lines were similarly deemed culpable for any vehicle that was in excess of fifty percent complete and stationary.

As the number of convictions grew to millions, daily, even the reassignment of all government employees to deal with the ensuing documentary administration began to prove inadequate. Thence came Commander Booker's final stroke of mathematical genius. He argued that as all vehicle owners were, on average, fined for parking violations two hundred times in each day, this average number of offences could simply be assumed, and the resultant fines added to vehicle road tax. Thus the statistics for solved crimes would be maintained without the need to directly enforce the law on the streets. This also avoided the unnecessary expense and logistical complications of maintaining a police force.

Anecdotally there has been some public concern about a perceived dramatic increase in murder, rape, armed robbery and terrorist offences - also gridlock caused in most towns by indiscriminate parking. Britain can be proud, however, that, statistically speaking, crime is no longer a problem.

~*~*~*~*~

Helping the Police with their Enquiries

A relative of mine works at Scotland Yard. I was delighted when he invited me to tour this icon of crime detection and learn of modern police practice.

I marvelled at computers, state-of-the-art laboratories and the air of efficiency as officers hurried purposefully back and forth - presumably delivering critical pieces of case solving information.

'I'm amazed that all criminals aren't instantly banged to rights,' I enthused.

Henry sighed. 'None of it seems to help us much,' he confided in a whisper.

I was puzzled. 'But Scotland Yard has a crime detection rate envied by the world?'

'Come with me.' Henry turned down a dimly lit corridor. 'Remember,' he continued with earnest sincerity, 'everything is in the strictest confidence.'

I followed him to a door at the end of the corridor. We entered an Edwardian styled drawing room. An old lady with greying hair and seated on a sofa, looked up whilst pouring tea.

'Ah, Chief Inspector,' she said to Henry, 'would you and your guest care for some Assam?'

Henry introduced Dorothy. Other older people sat in armchairs or paced the floor, deep in thought.

'I'm glad you dropped by,' said Dorothy to Henry. 'I've been thinking about the Regent's Park Murder. It's clear that the victim was strangled by an orang-utan, clubbed by a gorilla and finally smothered with the fur of a baboon. The deceased was also the recently spurned gay lover of the head keeper of primates at London Zoo.'

'So *he* did it,' Henry concluded with amazement. 'We never had an inkling. We've been concentrating our enquiries on shepherds in the Orkneys.'

Dorothy cast a puzzled glance at Henry. 'However, I discovered that a cousin of the victim bore a grudge over an inheritance which finally drove her to murder!'

Henry gasped. 'However did you deduce that?'

'It was the final words of the victim,' Dorothy revealed. 'He said he'd been murdered by his cousin due to a grudge over an inheritance.'

'We shouldn't have ignored that clue,' sighed Henry, using his mobile to brief the investigation team.

Dorothy addressed me. 'You seem confused, Mr Morrison?'

I gestured around me. 'I don't see where all this fits with Scotland Yard?'

'It's been known for over a century,' Dorothy explained, 'that police are incapable of detecting crime. Fortunately, that skill has remained amongst a small group of smug, amateur, upper class pensioners. This remains a closely guarded secret. The crime historian, Agatha Christie, was only allowed to publish by pretending Marple and Poirot were fictitious.'

I was incredulous. 'So you, and others like you, solve all crimes?'

'Yes. Mostly we review evidence collected by the police. If crimes are committed by the upper classes at country houses, of course, one of us is usually a guest at the time, so that facilitates those investigations.' Dorothy gestured towards the adjoining room. 'We undertake denouements in the library. Suspects question why they must dress for dinner and then hold gin and tonics while one of us expounds details of the crime. The guilty are always so impressed, however, by exact analyses of their motives and actions that they immediately confess.'

I was fascinated by crime detection, and now I knew how it was done.

~*~*~*~

Quantitative Easing

UK – March 2009:
The Bank of England is to expand the amount of money in the system by £75bn in an attempt to boost bank lending - a process known as 'quantitative easing'. This is, in effect, printing money.'

~**~

To:
Mr Mervyn King
Governor of The Bank of England,
Bank of England,
Threadneedle Street,
London,
EC2R 8AH

From:
Swan and Millicent Morrison

15th March 2009

Dear Mr Mervyn King,

My wife and I have been noting with concern news reports about problems with the world's economy.

Fortunately, we have modest savings and a frugal lifestyle and so, thus far, have been largely unaffected by the global economic downturn. We are very worried, however, about the effect on younger people who are threatened with redundancy, debt and repossession.

We are not very knowledgeable about financial matters, and so do not really understand what has caused the current recession. We have gathered from the news, however, that matters would be improved if people spent more money, and we understand that you are printing additional bank notes for that purpose.

Although Millie and I are just ordinary pensioners, we would like to 'do our bit' as our parents did in 1939.

If you would like to send us some of the extra money you are printing, we would be very happy to spend every penny in the High Street for you.

We have thought about what we might do with such purchases, as Millie and I do not want for much. We are involved with a number of local charities and plan to dispose of some items to those causes. Millie has also tidied our spare bedroom to store the remaining goods while we decide what to do with them.

Unfortunately, as we live in a small pensioners' flat, the spare bedroom is not very big, and we need to use it when our son comes to stay. We wondered, therefore, when you send the money, if you could advise on smaller, high value products, the purchase of which would most benefit the British economy.

We thought that one million pounds might be a useful initial sum. This probably appears as insignificant loose change to you compared to the amount of money that you are hoping to pump into the economy, or that has been casually lost by the banking industry. Millie is worried, however, about the practicalities of getting thousands of pounds worth of goods home from Argos, and so, if it's OK with you, we would like to see how we get on before committing ourselves to spending more.

We would also like to reassure you that you can count upon our total discretion in this matter, and that we are proposing this scheme not for our own personal gain, but for England!

Yours sincerely,

Swan and Millicent Morrison.

~*~*~*~

Guantánamo Bay

Chalet 27
Guantánamo Bay Resort
Guantánamo Province
Cuba

Dear Mick,

I hope your new job is going well.

As you know, our whole family was delighted when you got that high profile post to monitor the behaviour standards of politically influential people in the UK. We realised at the time that *you'd* need to be seen as beyond reproach. However, some of us were very surprised and worried when we learned that all your close relatives would also be positively vetted to check that none of us might potentially cause media embarrassment.

Our worst fears seemed confirmed when Aunt Mary, brother-in-law George, sister Audrey and I were arrested by Special Branch, driven to Brize Norton and bundled onto an American Air Force plane.

One of our guards then let slip that we were heading for internment at Guantánamo Bay.

Aunt Mary was stoical. She reasoned that it would be damaging for you if the press learned of her thirty years as a hooker. Also she was relieved to get away from all those people hounding her for the thousands she owed in gambling debts.

George was less resigned. Although he'd spent years in prison for burglary, he'd heard that everyone got regular electric shocks to their private parts in Guantánamo and was worried how that would affect his prostate problem.

Audrey tried to be encouraging, pointing out that mains voltage in Cuba was only 110 volts as compared to 240 volts in the UK, but I knew she was anxious too. Due to the speed at which we'd left the UK, she'd made no arrangements to look after the cannabis factory in her cellar.

Initially, I wondered why they'd arrested me. OK, I drink too much, and you've fairly described me as a con artist and serial adulterer, but that didn't make me any different from the MPs and senior public figures you'd be investigating.

Aunt Mary thought that was probably the point. She said they'd created your job to stop people who should be setting a public example from behaving with less honesty, integrity and morality than the lowest of us plebs. The public were sick of those at the top thinking they'd got a divine right to get away with bloody anything and treat the rest of us with contempt.

It was then that an officer came to talk to us. He explained what we'd already guessed: We were being kept out of the way so we couldn't be an embarrassment until you moved on from your job. It appeared, however, that they'd closed Guantánamo Bay as a detention and interrogation camp. They'd reopened it specifically as a secret internment resort for politically embarrassing relatives of honest and decent British and American public figures.

It's now like an all-expenses-paid holiday camp. They've replaced water boarding with water skiing, and the only torture is watching American TV – and that's optional.

As I sit here watching the sun set over the Caribbean, sipping a Cuban rum cocktail and smoking an Havana cigar, I can reassure you that I'm very pleased with the way things have turned out. Aunt Mary, George and Audrey also send their best wishes and say there's no need for you to rush to change jobs.

Your favourite brother,
Arthur.

~*~*~*~

8 – Health and Social Care

Bananas

Safety Warning and Urgent Recall Notice:

The Short Humour story that previously appeared on this page has been withdrawn by order of the Police.

If you have this story in an earlier edition of this book or have downloaded a copy from *the Short Humour Site*, please do not read it or re-read it. Delete it from your computer, and take to your nearest police station any printed or removable media on which it is stored.

It has come to light that the story, called *Bananas*, by Swan Morrison, was, inadvertently, the funniest piece of humour ever written. In susceptible individuals such writing can trigger uncontrollable and unstoppable laughter. It is impossible to eat or drink whilst convulsed with such humorous hysteria, hence there is serious risk of death within five or six days. There is currently no known treatment, and those affected have been maintained under sedation in hospital.

Similar pieces of writing have been developed by intelligence services in Russia and in the West. Indeed, it is believed that the murder of at least one former KGB agent was effected by inducing 'Mirthus Gravis' from reading such a story passed to him in a London restaurant. This was discovered when staff in the restaurant, who had seen parts of the text over his shoulder, tested positive for pathological joviality.

The Government employs teams of brilliant comedians to undertake the secret and dangerous research into this material, despite this leaving those who are less funny, or not funny at all, to fill comedy entertainment roles in the media. Even with such research, however, the most deadly humour is often found by chance. National disaster was narrowly averted in the UK just prior to a party political broadcast by the Leader of the Opposition. On analysis of his speech it was clear that hearing his plans for governing the country could have left over eighty percent of the population in agonising contortions of laughter. Fortunately, the danger was identified in time, and all subsequent policy statements have been sufficiently bland and substanceless to be safe – even for children.

A particular danger of the Swan Morrison story was that it appeared to maintain its potency in translation. Even Germans reported a strange and unfamiliar sensation on reading it, together with an involuntary vocalisation, sounding something like: 'Ha Ha'. This contributed to the fear that the material might fall into the hands of terrorists. This story read on national radio could have a destructive power equivalent to ten megapaxmans – one paxman being the effect on an evasive politician of a TV interview during the UK current affairs programme, *Newsnight*. It would also, of course, be fatal to the reader, but 'suicide humorous story reading' is an ever-present risk.

In addition to research for military purposes, work continues on the use of deadly humour to control vermin. Oxford University has built a facility to discover what rats find amusing – a move that has led to some confusion among anti-vivisectionists. So far, the one about the two mice and the gerbil is said to be showing promise.

Finally, although the story on this page has been removed, some people may be affected by other writing in this book. If you find that you have been unable to stop laughing for more than twelve consecutive hours, consult your doctor immediately.

POLICE   POLICE   POLICE

~*~*~*~

Casketech

You may have read of the horrific experiences of those pronounced dead in hospital only to recover consciousness in the hospital mortuary.

Hospitals have since worked hard to improve staff discipline to ensure that patients are not declared dead simply because they have annoyed nursing staff or because their consultants have wished to leave early for the day. Nevertheless, public confidence has been shaken, and demand has arisen for fail-safe systems to avoid the risk of being buried or cremated alive.

My company, Casketech, has reacted to this by manufacturing hi-tech coffins with an eye to this NQDY (Not Quite Dead Yet) market.

The personal inconvenience of live burial was recognised in the Victorian era, and mechanical signalling apparatus was devised to allow coffin occupants to communicate with those six feet above. In this modern age, the preference has been for more sophisticated technology.

Our *Cadaver Communicator* range has become very popular, featuring, as it does, telephone, fax and broadband Internet connection. Top of the range models are also equipped with satellite television and a computer games console to pass the time whilst awaiting disinterment.

Taking such technology to the grave has also prompted developments in Spiritualist Churches, which now routinely hold e-seances. This is despite some cases of unfortunate and tragic confusion between communication from *beyond* the grave and communication from *within* it.

Those not reassured by our products alone can engage a 'personal burial consultant'. Such advisors are interred with the suspected deceased and observe them until a confirmatory level of decomposition had occurred. Coffins to allow such a precaution need, of course, to be equipped with air, water and food supplies, together with cooking, bathroom and sleeping facilities. Some of our deluxe models are now being resold as low cost housing despite the alarm initially caused by people emerging from the ground in cemeteries. Fundamentalist Christians were particularly disappointed when it was clarified that this behaviour did not herald Judgement Day.

Coffins for cremations have posed particular design problems. Cremations do not allow the luxury of time for communication and rescue afforded by conventional burial, and so the emphasis must be on rapid escape.

One of the earlier designs from our *Get Up And Go* range incorporated technology derived from the ejection seat of the F-111 fighter-bomber. The provisionally departed were, of course, fully equipped with protective clothing and a crash helmet.

In the case of a real revival, the congregation and church authorities might well consider any collateral damage to be a small price to pay for a family to be reunited with a loved one. Some faulty release mechanisms, however, led to several individuals, who had genuinely passed over, dramatically leaving their memorial services.

The televised flight of a much-respected dignitary from his coffin in the aisle of Westminster Abbey, through the North Rose Window, over the Houses of Parliament and into the Thames was one such example. Fortunately, the sudden inspiration of the Archbishop of Canterbury to conduct the proceedings as a burial at sea was a masterstroke of improvisation that saved the day.

Finally, remember our billboard advert which is totally black except for a speech bubble which reads 'I wish I'd gone to Casketech!!'. Come and see us before it's too late.

~*~*~*~*~

Driving Round the Bend

Now I am in my late nineties,
My memory's got rather poor.
Like why am I driving out into the night
Away from my own garage door?

I seem to be driving the car very fast,
But the switch for the lights I can't find.
That's not a significant problem to me -
Being almost totally blind.

There's bumping and thumping and squelching,
And I think I can hear people's screams.
It's all rather odd and confusing;
I do wish I knew what it means.

I stand by my car in my garage.
I cannot remember quite why.
I'd best close the doors and go up to bed;
There's the moon and the stars in the sky.

My daughter has called round to see me;
Must be morning - Yes, outside it's light.
She tells me the 'Hit and Run Madman'
Claimed fifteen more victims last night.

The first four were hit on the pavements -
Such carnage police hadn't seen.
Five chased from the road 'cross the golf course;
Mowed down on the seventeenth green.

Three more were hit in their gardens
As they went out to call in the cat.
The ones who left open the patio doors
Were run down in their lounge where they sat.

Such stories of death and destruction
Give us poor, frail, old folk a fright.
I'm just glad that I'm too disabled
To dare venture outside at night.

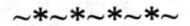

~*~*~*~*~

Sequencing the Genome

'Hello, Doctor. I gather you've got my test results?'

'Yes, Mr Morrison. Please sit down. Here's the printout of your genetic code, your genome.'

'What does it all mean?'

'Well, our genetic code is the blueprint for how our bodies are made. Once, it took years to get this information. Now we can obtain a complete genome in ten minutes from just one strand of hair. It tells us if patients are at risk of developing certain medical conditions. Treatments or lifestyle changes can then be recommended to reduce risks.'

'What have you found from mine?'

'Well, you've genes that cause fat, sugar and salt to be metabolised unusually quickly. That means it's important you eat a lot of takeaways, cakes, chocolate and snack foods. It would also be best to avoid vegetables.'

'I see. Are there other lifestyle factors I should bear in mind?'

'How much alcohol do you drink?'

'Two glasses of wine a night.'

'That's probably not enough. You've genes which lead to over-activity of the liver. It's important to give the liver lots to do. Processing alcohol is particularly beneficial.'

'How much should I drink?'

'A wine box a day. Perhaps a few beers and the odd scotch too - just to be safe.'

'That sounds expensive.'

'Don't worry. Due to your medical condition, wine, beer and spirits can be supplied free by the National Heath Service. Just order them at the pharmacy as you leave. They'll deliver to your door.'

'What are the genes marked on the chart in red?'

'I'm afraid they're a particular problem. You're at very high risk of difficulties in the genital region.'

'That sounds worrying. Is there any treatment?'

'There's one very effective therapy, but it requires you to have very regular sex with a constant stream of attractive young women. Once again, don't worry. We can arrange for these to be provided free by the NHS. Here's a catalogue.'

'My wife may object.'

'Yes, partners sometimes initially raise some concerns, but our community nurse can assist her in coming to terms with your therapy. Also, there are support groups.'

'Is that everything?'

'Not quite. You could be prone to problems with the muscles that control your eyes. It's important that they undertake sufficient movement, but it's also critical to avoid tiring yourself with unnecessary exercise. We often recommend staying in bed until at least lunchtime every day whilst watching football on TV - Sky sports channels are available on prescription. That also provides an excellent opportunity to administer medicinal alcohol and undertake sexual therapy.'

'My employer might have a problem with all that time away from work.'

'I can sign a certificate so your boss allows you time off for treatment. You have a right to expect support for your disabilities. With your complex medical problems, you'll need understanding and sympathy from everyone, possibly for years. Do you think you'll be able to cope with the treatments and lifestyle demands?'

'Well, spookily, I already engage in some, and I've thought I'd like to try the others.'

'It's remarkable how the body sometimes unconsciously knows what it needs. If you stick to the regime, you'll have a very good prognosis.'

'Thank you, Doctor. I'll do my best. Good day.'

~*~*~*~*~

The Well Women's Group

Jennifer was last to arrive at the monthly social gathering of the Well Women's Group.

'Hi,' she said as she joined the other super-fit paragons of health and vitality.

'How are you?' responded Sarah, handing Jennifer an isotonic, vitamin enhanced fruit juice.

'I feel great, as usual,' Jennifer replied, 'but I'm pretty pissed-off.'

Alice joined them, jogging on the spot. 'What's the matter, Jen?'

'I'm sick of being exploited by members of the ill community just because of my continuous wellness.' Jennifer sipped her drink. 'Mavis, who works with me, got run over by a bus on Monday. Now I've got to do all her work as well as my own while she just lies in a hospital bed for a year or two.'

'I know just what you mean,' Sarah sympathised. 'That selfish son of a bitch who was painting my flat couldn't even go on holiday to Africa without catching Ebola. I bet the shit gave no thought to having left the work half finished and me having all the hassle of finding another decorator…'

'At least you can see real symptoms of physical illnesses,' Alice interrupted. 'It's the malingering sods with so called mental illnesses that make me so angry. Those idle bastards just whinge that they are suffering from depression, or similar, and expect the rest of us to sympathetically let them freeload.'

'You ex-husband had depression, didn't he, Alice?' remembered Jennifer.

'As soon as he told me, I said I was divorcing him.'

Sarah poured herself another juice. 'How did he react to that?'

'When that type don't get a guilt free passport to pampered luxury, they up the stakes. My ex said he would kill himself.'

Jennifer was curious. 'Why do people do that?'

'They're angry about not being able to manipulate everyone,' explained Alice, 'and want to punish us all with guilt.'

'What did you do when he made that threat?' asked Sarah.

'I bought some rope, sharpened the knives and left full boxes of paracetemol around the house. I even got some new cartridges for his shotgun. Then I walked out.

'Did he...?' continued Sarah, wide-eyed.

'Nope. In the end I had to shoot him myself.'

Suddenly, the attention of the three women was drawn to Marilyn as she staggered half way across the room and then collapsed to the floor in front of them.

'She doesn't look well,' observed Jennifer, noting the rapid, shallow breathing, dilated pupils and blue-tinged skin tone.

The women recognised a medical emergency and knew they must act quickly.

Sarah and Jennifer lifted Marilyn and carried her towards the door. Alice recovered Marilyn's handbag and, while following the others, removed Marilyn's Well Women's Group membership card from her bag.

They deposited the body on the doorstep of a house across the road, rang the bell and ran.

Back at the Group, Jennifer poured juice for them all. 'The nerve of that woman,' she said. 'She'll get a final formal warning from the Group if she lives.'

'And if she dies?' enquired Sarah.

Jennifer and Alice spoke decisively in unison: 'Exclusion for gross misconduct.'

~*~*~*~*~

The Sickness Advisor

'Hello Doreen. Thanks for coming to see me. Please sit down.'

'If it's about my sickness record in this company, I want my Union rep present.'

'Well, it is about your absences, but not in any critical way.'

'What do you mean?'

'I've become very concerned about how little time off sick our other employees take. They appear to be excessively dedicated to the Company. Jones from Finance came to work last week with flu symptoms, and I had to order him to go home when he collapsed at his desk.'

'What's that got to do with me?'

'I think other staff have had too little practice in being ill and don't know how to deal with it. You, on the other hand, have enormous experience of taking sick leave, and I thought you might be able to advise your colleagues.'

'What could I tell them?'

'For example, you seem able to detect the onset of physical and psychological maladies long before you show any symptoms, sometimes weeks before. Your use of preventative sick leave to forestall further development of an illness is truly innovative. Indeed, I consider myself most fortunate that you can join me here today.'

'I see.'

'The therapeutic approaches you use to promote your recovery are also an example to all.'

'What therapeutic approaches?'

'The late night clubbing is one example. Also, I gather you convalesced in Benidorm when you were stricken with last month's disabling condition.'

'Who told you about that?'

'It doesn't matter. The important thing is that you've just the practical expertise that this company needs.'

'What do you want me to do?'

'Give regular lectures to staff about identification of illness and how to give themselves the maximum possible time away from work to recover. Also, accepting the role as full time Company Sickness Advisor should enhance staff perceptions of you.'

'What staff perceptions?'

'There's a general scurrilous and defamatory misperception that you're a useless, idle malingerer. I think both you and your Union rep would wish the Company to take all possible measures to correct this. Your new high profile role in regularly telling staff full details of how you decide upon and manage your absences will afford you a new status.'

'I'm not doing that. That might reinforce the misperception that I'm a useless, idle malingerer, and devious and manipulative too!'

'I'm sorry to hear that as this task is well within your existing job description. Refusal to undertake it would force me to address the matter via a disciplinary route, probably resulting in dismissal.'

'I'm not waiting for the completion of a disciplinary process. I resign!'

'That's your decision, of course. You're an excellent employee and the Company will be very sorry to lose you. We will, of course, give you first class references, with no mention of your absence record - just like those bastards you previously worked for gave us.'

'What did you say?'

'I said we would give you first class references, with no mention of your sickness record – just like those bright stars you previously worked for gave us. We won't hold you to a notice period if you want to leave now.'

'Perhaps I'll go then. To be honest, I don't feel too good and was going to take a sickie this afternoon, anyway. Goodbye.'

~*~*~*~*~

The Conspiracy

I have always harboured reservations about adults convincing children of the existence of Santa Claus. Perhaps it is an innocent myth, but it requires lies from those trusted adults. I sometimes wonder how many young people experience a sense of betrayal on discovering the truth.

This moral dilemma posed by Santa occurs just annually. More frequently, social pressure forces collusion with a more heinous conspiracy.

The mandatory reaction when a young woman announces that she is expecting her first baby is as culturally prescribed and socially enforced as the requirement to ask a toddler about presents received from Father Christmas. In conversation with first time mums-to-be it is de rigueur to express excitement and delight and promote a fatuous, mythical belief that parenthood is simply wonderful.

'Why do we lie to them?' I asked a group of fellow parents when the latest victim of this subterfuge had left the staffroom. 'We've just told Janis that having a baby is going to be great and she'll really enjoy being a parent.' I shook my head in despair. 'We all know that she's really going to have at least twenty years of Hell: sleepless nights, poverty, massively restricted freedom, stress in her relationship which might break-up as a result, worry about finding good schools, conflict with argumentative youngsters and battles with bolshy, arrogant adolescents.'

'Swan's got a point,' conceded Julia. 'She's only at sixteen weeks. There's still time for a termination.'

'Why should *she* get away with it?' John said, angrily. 'No one warned *us*. Susan and I were told exactly the same misleading nonsense that we're feeding to Janis.'

'At least if she's got kids she won't have to face the covert hostility of other parents,' Sally reminded us. 'The couple next door to me chose not to have children. They spend their whole lives doing what they like and having fun. I hate them.'

'Bastards,' agreed Julia, thinking of the damage caused to her home last weekend during the fifteenth birthday party of her son.

'Of course I secretly do what I can to get even,' continued Sally. 'Damage to their cars, vandalism to their house, that sort of thing.'

'I think that those who choose not to have children should pay tax at ninety percent and spend eight months each year in a forced labour camp,' bemoaned John.

'Hear, hear,' everyone chorused.

I later encountered Janis in the car park. 'It's great for you that you're having a baby,' I lied. 'I bet it'll be fantastic.' A thought suddenly occurred to me. 'Did you believe in Father Christmas when you were a child?' I asked.

'Until I was ten,' Janis replied.

'How did you feel when you discovered that it wasn't true?'

'A bit disappointed,' she admitted. 'Still, it was fun while it lasted. As an adult you don't get the chance to live a fairytale. It's made me wiser though,' she joked. 'I'm not getting caught like that again!'

~*~*~*~

Ten

Rob parked his ambulance on the remote moorland road next to the twisted remains of a crash barrier. He grabbed his paramedic kit and rushed down the hillside to where the Mondeo had stopped on impact with a Rowan.

'My name's Rob, I'm a paramedic,' he said to the lone, male occupant of the vehicle. 'I need to check if you're injured.'

Shortly afterwards, Rob radioed the control room: 'Tango Bravo calling... One male occupant... No serious injuries... Trapped in vehicle...'

'Thanks Tango Bravo... Fire and Rescue ETA twenty minutes...'

Rob looked again at the victim and felt a faint sense of recognition. He took his personal PDA from his pocket. 'Can I check a few details while we wait?'

'Sure,' came the reply. 'It'll take my mind off all this'.

Rob took a name, address, date of birth and other information and fed the data into his computer.

It displayed: '1969 – Ten – No Details'.

Rob was astounded by the Ten.

To those around him, Rob appeared affable and mild mannered. He had never been known to lose his temper – whatever the provocation. This was because, since childhood, he had kept a record of injustices towards himself, together with details of their perpetrators. He then secretly selected and enacted appropriate retribution as circumstances allowed.

He assigned a number between one and ten to each offence. Offenders at Level One deserved some minor annoyance such as having their car aerials snapped off. Offences at Level Ten, however, demanded summary execution.

'1969' indicated the date of the affront. He used notebooks back then. When Rob had later compiled an electronic database, some paper records had been lost. Clearly no details remained of the 1969 offence. Nevertheless, it was unusual to forget the circumstances of a Ten.

Tens included the man who had run off with his wife and who had subsequently been killed in that unexplained gas explosion. Then there was his adulterous ex-wife, herself, who had been the tragic victim of a, never found, hit-and-run driver - and not forgetting the boss who fired him after ten loyal years at the meat packing factory; the one who had accidentally fallen into an industrial mincer.

'What were you doing in 1969?' Rob asked.

His patient thought this an odd question but concluded that Rob was trying to distract him with conversation. 'I was a traffic warden in Hammersmith.'

Rob had lived in Hammersmith in 1969, but his memory was not refreshed. Rob considered himself tough but fair: Parking tickets might warrant a One or a Two, but never a Ten.

The driver found that talking calmed his anxiety and continued to recount his life. He showed Rob family photographs from his wallet. Very rapidly Rob discovered much about his companion and, indeed, began to like him. The Ten, however, remained unexplained.

Rob heard sirens. Fire and Rescue would arrive shortly. He withdrew a syringe from his bag. 'This will calm you,' he said as he administered the injection.

Rob climbed to the road and met the rescue team. 'A delayed heart attack,' he said. 'Must have been the shock.'

Rob returned sadly to his ambulance. The accident victim had seemed a very nice chap, and Rob could still not recall their encounter in 1969.

A Ten, however, was a Ten.

~*~*~*~

9 – History and Heritage

The Olympian

(From an original idea by Alan Pinkett)

Peter greatly admired the achievements of British Olympians. He had watched the world beating performances of Sir Steve Redgrave, Linford Christie, Sally Gunnell and others and dreamed of one day joining their illustrious ranks. He imagined himself atop an Olympic podium, draped in a union flag, the notes of the British National Anthem drowned-out by cheers from a rapturous crowd.

There was, however, a problem. The great Olympians not only had outstanding aptitude for their sports but demonstrated unstinting dedication. His heroes and heroines had committed themselves to years of rigorous training in order to achieve their goals. Peter, by contrast, was disinclined to expend undue effort on his quest for Olympic glory.

It was to resolve this dilemma that Peter studied a list of Olympic sports in search of the least demanding.

He discarded activities requiring strength or physical fitness and thus focussed upon shooting events. Remaining still and gently squeezing a trigger certainly met his athletic criteria. In addition, one event seemed to offer a solution to the problem of training and practice – the Ten Metre Air Pistol*.

Peter opened the connecting door between his living room and kitchen and paced from his sofa. It was exactly ten metres to the kitchen wall. He had found his Olympic event.

Peter purchased an air pistol and began his Olympic preparations. Every day he would lay on the sofa watching TV, a Guinness in one hand, his pistol in the other. Previously he had resented long TV commercial breaks, particularly as he paid additional subscriptions for the adult channels. Now, these intermissions afforded an ideal opportunity to blast away at targets nailed to the kitchen wall.

Within a year, Peter's aim was so perfect that he decided to repair the peppered walls, ceilings, furniture and windows that testified to his earlier practice. He even replaced the cat.

Despite his proficiency at home, his first public competition was disappointing. Peter had missed with every shot and lost further points for accidentally despatching the host club's cat.

The problem was obvious: He was unused to firing whilst standing or when sober. With appropriate adjustments to technique, his next competition performance impressed all. There was little question that Peter was destined to represent Great Britain at the forthcoming Olympics.

~**~

Peter's team-mates carried his sofa into the Olympic arena and positioned his TV and DVD player.

As his Olympic competitors fired carefully aimed shots, Peter loaded his favourite *XXXBabes* DVD and downed his first can of Guinness.

Competitors were required to fire sixty shots within one hundred and five minutes. His team became increasingly anxious as Peter, having fired none, watched *Lesbian Lovers* to its end, leaving just one minute of the competition remaining.

Then, whilst finishing his tenth can of Guinness, Peter lifted his specially adapted semi-automatic air pistol and triumphantly fired sixty pellets into the targets' centres.

Peter felt dizzy as he stood on the podium waving his Olympic gold medal. Perhaps he should have postponed the additional celebratory drinks until after the ceremony? Nevertheless, as he fell backwards off the podium, wrapped in the union flag and with the sounds of British National Anthem and the cheers of the crowd in his ears, he entered the happiest state of alcoholic unconsciousness of his life.

~**~

*The Ten Metre Air Pistol is a genuine Olympic event.
If you read more about the event you will note that Peter's victory led to many changes in the rules of the sport.
These include firing from the standing position, loading only one pellet at a time and, most critically, all competitors being breathalysed.

~*~*~*~*~

The Picassos

The Museu Picasso in Barcelona appeared deserted as I admired *Science And Charity*.

I suddenly became aware of an old man beside me, also studying the painting.

'Picasso was a fine artist,' I ventured.

'Indeed,' my companion concurred. 'His death from scarlet fever in 1898 was a tragedy.'

'Picasso died in 1973,' I corrected.

The stranger was silent for some moments. 'Follow me,' he said.

He led to *Carrer De La Riera De Sant Joan, From The Window Of The Artist's Studio* and pointed at the random, shapeless daubs of black and brown paint. 'Does this look like it was painted by the same person?'

It was certainly radically different in style. 'Surely there was just one Picasso?' I queried.

My guide shook his head. 'After his success at the National Fine Arts Exhibition in Madrid in 1897 powerful people recognised Picasso's future financial potential. When he died they formed a secret brotherhood to conceal the death.'

'How could that be done?'

The old man beckoned onwards to *Portrait Of The Writer Ramon Raventós* and *The Embrace*. 'These are by a young unknown who closely resembled Picasso. The Brotherhood found him in Horta de Sant Joan.'

I looked closely at the paintings. 'They aren't so accomplished.'

'Sadly, he had little time to improve before he was struck by lightning near Madrid in 1901.'

My companion moved to *The Madman*. 'This is a self portrait of his replacement. They discovered him in a Paris lunatic asylum.'

'He showed talent,' I observed.

'Unfortunately the voices in his head kept commanding him to buy blue paint. His apartment was stacked from floor to ceiling.'

My informant gestured towards *The Forsaken*. 'And he insisted on painting such miserable, depressing works with it.'

'What became of him?' I enquired.

'Collapsing crates of his blue paint crushed him to death in 1905. They couldn't clean all the pigment from the body. He was bright turquoise in his casket.'

'And *his* successor?'

'An inspired artist, but rapid onset macular degeneration led to virtual blindness by 1917. He then developed Parkinson's disease.'

We continued past canvasses depicting misplaced and disconnected features characteristic of paintings by a blind person who lacked muscle control.

The old man paused again at *Portrait Of Jaume Sabarés With Ruff And Hat*. 'He completed this just before he died in London in 1939.'

'This one died too?'

'An inexperienced helper was pushing his wheelchair across a railway level crossing…'

'Four Picassos dead?'

'The Brotherhood named it "The Curse of the Picassos". They chose to not recruit another.'

'Who undertook later works?'

'Members of the Brotherhood or their relatives. None had any artistic talent but, by that time, anything with "Picasso" written on it was hailed as a masterpiece and work of genius. They employed an actor for photographs and public appearances.'

We stopped at *The Pigeons*. 'I particularly like this one,' continued the old man. 'It was done by the five year old granddaughter of one of the Brotherhood. She meant them to be doves but couldn't get the tails right.'

We finally arrived at the gallery containing the interpretations of the Velázquez masterpiece, *Las Meninas*.

My companion gestured at the paintings. 'By now, the Brotherhood had removed the C, A and O from Picasso and were taking the other four letters with a vengeance.'

I closely examined the childlike scrawls and scribblings on several pieces. It was clear that my guide was telling the truth. 'How do you know all this?' I asked.

I turned around. The old man had vanished as quickly and silently as he had appeared.

I left the museum past a photograph of the Picasso of later years. He bore a remarkable resemblance to my recent companion and had the same bright eyes and mischievous smile.

As I glanced back at that picture, I even believe he winked.

~*~*~*~

The Araf and the Ildiwch

In the wilds of Western Wales
Mythic creatures still abound,
Whose names, for information,
On the road signs can be found.

The Araf is a vocal beast.
Hills echo with his call.
He looks quite like a womble,
Though he's all of twelve feet tall.

To visitors his risk is small.
Say 'boo', and he will go.
But never will he rush himself,
Thus signs warn: 'Araf Slow'.

The Ildiwch is dangerous.
He's teeth and spines and claws.
He'll not care for your safety
Nor for any human laws.

It's very best to follow
The advice the road signs say:
If you chance upon an Ildiwch
Don't cross his path, Give Way!

Traeth are aquatic mammals
With green fur and huge blue feet.
They live in social colonies
Where many thousands meet.

As a protected species,
Habitats are out of reach.
A conservation sanctuary
Is often marked 'Traeth Beach'.

Llwybr Cyhoeddus are rodents
Who excavate burrows in the ground.
But despite fluorescent ears and tails
They're very rarely found.

So if this timid animal
Might just be there to see,
It's announced on Public Footpath signs
In the vicinity.

Strange beasties roam this ancient land:
Rhybudd and Arafwch Nawr,
Gorsaf, Gyrrwch yn ofalus
And very many more.

You too can see this fauna.
Close searching rarely fails.
Just watch out for the signposts
As you journey into Wales.

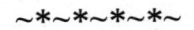

~*~*~*~

I Guess that's Why They Call It the Blues

On the porch of his shack in the Mississippi Delta
Blind Willie McSmith picked guitar.
A pattern evolved from his musical experiments
With a beauty beyond tunes thus far.

Had Willie McSmith had some musical understanding
Of this 'Shit hot tune of mine',
He might have explained its harmonic progression
Of twelve bars in 4/4 time.

He tried to establish a suitable name:
A label the whole world could see.
He chose to assign it 'The Oranges'-
Nearby was a large citrus tree.

It's a curious feature of nature
That one not infrequently finds
Original thoughts independently
Occurring to several minds.

So it was that Blind Reverend Sammy McJones,
On a porch just a few miles away,
Came upon the identical 'Crap cool notes'
On precisely the same summer's day.

Blind Sammy, he also considered a name
For this top of his musical cream.
He selected 'The Blues' from some English connections
To Chelsea Football Team.

Then Sammy McJones, he began to compose
And was spoilt by the rhymes he could choose.
Clues, cruise, hues, shoes, use, dues and news:
Great cues rhyme and fuse with The Blues.

Soon the form spread on outwards from Sammy's own porch
To New Orleans, then on to you.
Inspiring jazz, rock and roll, heavy metal
And hip hop - to name but a few.

Blind Willie McSmith, he attempted to write,
But couldn't complete his first song.
What on Earth could he rhyme with 'The Oranges'?
There was something quite desperately wrong.

At the head of his grave in the Mississippi Delta
Willie's last words are carved for all times:
'If ya finds a shit hot new way to play yer guitar,
Call it after a color that rhymes'.

~*~*~*~

There'll be Bluebirds over the White Cliffs of Dover

George felt overwhelmed with helplessness. It was the 3rd September 2004 and he calculated that a further five years, six months and eight days of pointless, twenty-first century, employment-related stress remained before retirement.

He recalled his grandfather's description of this identical feeling when, exactly sixty-five years before, Churchill had announced the declaration of war. A brief calculation confirmed the further coincidence that George's remaining servitude precisely spanned the duration of that war.

He found himself humming *There'll be Bluebirds over the White Cliffs of Dover* as he devised a plan to emulate the coping mechanisms that had sustained his grandfather through those previous dark times.

In George's mind, the recent departmental reorganisation and sudden introduction of new management mingled with the Nazi invasion of Poland. That weekend, he constructed an Anderson shelter in his garden. Though wartime rations were meagre, he was relieved that Tesco had all commodities in stock and there were no significant queues.

He sought reassurance in recorded speeches by Prime Minister Churchill. The Blitz, however, was relentless: Government guidelines and EU directives rained down with devastating effect. Jones from Finance and Richardson from Highways were both escorted from the council offices in straightjackets - a tragic loss of brave comrades. George reflected that had he not spent every night in his Anderson shelter wearing his gas mask and taking solace from Vera Lynn recordings, he too might have gone mad.

His blackout curtains gave passers-by the impression of great commitment to energy conservation. Neighbours also commended George on his environmental awareness as he dug his garden for victory. The park railings were never recovered.

He ordered facsimile copies of a wartime newspaper to be delivered on corresponding days. Each morning he avidly scoured the pages for news of Allied success.

The challenge by the Local Government Expeditionary Force against destruction of pensions and conditions of service gave hope. Although a military defeat, the heroic evacuation of Dunkirk rallied morale and allowed Union activists to regroup to fight another day.

The newspaper maintained an optimistic stance, although George knew morale on the Home Front was low. Increasing numbers of colleagues remained on long term stress-related sick leave. Mavis in Supplies enquired how George maintained his optimism. 'It's the end of the beginning,' he enigmatically replied - reflecting on that morning's news of Montgomery's victory at El Alamein.

Heinrich Bauer in Highways was clearly a German spy. Brazen too - he made no secret of being a native Berliner. George commenced covert operations by feeding Heinrich subtly inaccurate information - leading ultimately to the new M27 link road being constructed over a cliff, into the sea.

The success of the Normandy landings encouraged George that the end was near.

As the Second Army crossed the Rhine, work colleagues enquired about his preferred retirement celebration. All enthusiastically supported his suggestion of a street party reminiscent of VE day.

The 7th May 2010 was the greatest day of his life - a marvellous retirement party and Germany's unconditional surrender.

Now was time for rest, but not for too long. Experience with Heinrich had given George a taste for covert operations, and he had already compiled a list of those locally with Russian sounding names.

The Cold War had begun.

~*~*~*~

Top Tips for Travellers to England

'Happy is England! I could be content to see no other verdure than its own'
John Keats, 1817

We hope you enjoy your first English holiday. But be aware that culture and customs will differ from those at home.

Clothing:
When visiting a large metropolis, such as London or Manchester, you will need, in addition to normal clothing, a *kevlar* jacket. These provide protection against knives and some munitions. Cautious travellers might try a helmet and shield. In major cities, an upgrade of your hire car to an armoured troop carrier may afford greater peace of mind.

Etiquette:
By law, everyone in England must stop for tea at 4.00 pm each day. On hearing the siren, calmly retire to the nearest teashop. Remember that failure to pour the milk prior to pouring the tea can incur a hefty fine!

Why not join a queue? There will often be one available, but if you are with a party, you might like to form your own - simply line up behind one another.

It is customary to hand you wallet or handbag to any young person with a gun.

Food and Drink:
Exploit opportunities to sample traditional English fare. In restaurants, ask for 'a Chinese' or 'an Indian' - the latter being traditionally eaten after ten pints of extra strength Danish lager. You might also enjoy a pizza or a kebab.

The famed English 'Fish and Chips' comprises otherwise healthy fish and potatoes cocooned in deadly saturated fats. If etiquette demands acceptance of this dish, it is best dropped on the nearest pavement. The English adopt this practice, and streets on Friday and Saturday evenings are often strewn with discarded food together with comatose drunks and those who, following consumption of 'Fish and Chips', have experienced fatal heart attacks.

Language:

English learned at home will be of little value. English people, with the exception of the Queen and some BBC newsreaders, do not speak English. If you intend to converse with the locals, then learn translations such as:

Yes: *'Bleedin' might as well.'*
No: *'Who're you fuckin' kiddin'?'*

There are no equivalent words or expressions in modern conversational English for 'Please' or 'Thank you'.

Conversation:

All English conversation must include reference to the weather. This can be a helpful conversation starter - for example, you might state: 'What ho, it is warm/cool for this time of year, don't you think?' Remember that such references must be made in ALL circumstances or it is considered to be 'bad form'. If you assist in a rescue at one of the road traffic accidents you will encounter, you might comment: 'It is a particularly inclement evening to be pulled from the burning wreckage of your vehicle, do you not agree?' and perhaps add: 'Stiff upper lip, now. Pip, pip.'

Sport:

The English national sport is, of course, football. Rules are simple in that gangs of 'fans' wander the streets in a state of intoxication with the intent to kill rival 'fans' and 'foreigners'. You will fall within the definition of a 'foreigner', so this sport is best avoided.

Shopping and Souvenirs:

England is famous for its illicit drugs, and don't forget the exceptional value afforded by eastern European prostitution!!

Finally:

Enjoy the land of Shakespeare, Milton, The Kray Twins and The Yorkshire Ripper.

~*~*~*~*~

How Things Might Have Been

It is a great privilege to be Chief of the Western American Federation of Indian Tribes. I write these words while sitting on a high point in the foothills of the Sierra Nevada and looking down upon the lands of my peoples. Below are scattered many villages with traditional roundhouses and bark dwellings. I can see fields of oak, the acorns from which have provided sustenance for eight thousand years. Women are grinding acorn flour and small groups of men are setting-out to hunt.

I am proud of the survival of our traditional lifestyle. I feel more proud, however, that our philosophy of respect for all life and harmony with nature has spread throughout the world, leading to peace on Earth - something for which the whole planet now gives thanks to our legendary chief, White Flame.

All are taught of how, four thousand years ago, White Flame became Chief of my people. He too had rejoiced in their simple, peaceful and sustainable lifestyle. He had feared, however, that, one day, bad people might come from across the mountains and do us harm. White Flame had thus decreed that our most able men and women should devote some of their time to scientific and technological development.

Their fellows soon reaped the benefits as the wheel and the discovery of metal production enhanced their lives. So it was with other machines, the horseless carriage, the aeroplane, nuclear power, computers and myriad other advances culminating in intergalactic space travel. All were developed in research establishments while our traditional village lifestyle, the bedrock of our attitudes and philosophy, has quietly continued.

The great wisdom of White Flame was profoundly illustrated just one hundred and fifty years ago when bad men finally came from across the mountains. They wanted to take our gold – gold that we needed for advanced microprocessor circuitry. Thus their initial offers of beads, mirrors and whisky for our land seemed somewhat inadequate. When refused, however, they quickly reverted to threats of violence.

Fortunately, despite their huge numbers, greed, aggression and racism, their weaponry was no match for non-lethal defensive force-fields deployed from our anti-matter powered spacecraft.

We had no wish to interfere in the lives and cultures of others with whom we shared this planet. However, we felt that their propensity for killing each other in astronomical numbers for no particular reason was not a helpful trait. Neither was their apparent intent to destroy as quickly as possible all the resources of the Earth that my people had, for countless generations, honoured and cherished.

We, therefore, restrained them from the worst manifestations of their behaviour for four generations. By that time, their actions were no longer poisonously driven by memories of past cycles of violence. Hence we came to the peace and harmony of the world as it is today.

Sometimes I wonder what the world would have been like had it not been for White Flame. What would have happened if my people had simply sat on their backsides, grinding acorns and hunter-gathering for eight thousand years without any noticeable scientific or technological advancement?

A cold shiver runs down my spine when I think of how things might have been.

~*~*~*~*~

El Torero

Manuel Espadachín Torero strode proudly into the arena. He glanced at the terraced seating from which, as a child, he had gasped at the skill and bravery of his grandfather. Abuelito would taunt his bull and then deftly, at the final moment, avoid the path of the charging, enraged animal - flamboyantly swirling his cape, pass after pass, until the great beast was exhausted. His sword would then be thrust with surgical precision into the heart of the brave creature.

Manuel recalled the roar of the crowd, a turbulent sea of their waving white handkerchiefs and gracious acceptance by his grandfather of ears and tail cut from the noble vanquished.

He also remembered discontent, even then, from those who viewed this spectacle as a cruel and unnecessary part of Spanish culture. With time, those voices became louder until, with his father as matador, the final act of the historic art form was played out at a slaughterhouse away from public view.

From this small compromise, emboldened reformers drove even more rapid and radical change. Soon bulls could no longer be killed or even injured. The task of the picadores, banderilleros and matadors became to ensure the enjoyment of animals by offering favourite foods or ensuring they were comfortably shaded.

Further concerns were raised, however, by the tragic death of Manuel's father - fatally gored while giving a relaxing shoulder massage to a particularly tense Toro Bravo. It was feared that the creature might realise it had caused death and suffer irreparable psychological damage.

As an emergency measure, Jersey Meadows, Cattle Psychologist to the Stars, was flown from Hollywood to ensure expert treatment should the poor creature exhibit signs of Bovine Post-Traumatic Stress Disorder.

Clearly, however, a new species of animal was needed that was totally safe and whose happiness could be precisely gauged.

The Ragdoll cat was the unmistakable choice. Large and placid, these beautiful felines possess an unusual vocal range. Many incremental degrees of pleasure can be discerned, ranging from a relaxed meow of contentment to the dynamic purr of ecstasy – the goal of the modern contest.

So it was that Manuel sat in the raised armchair at the centre of the Plaza de Gatos. He summoned a banderilleo to bring Muffin, the Ragdoll cat, and place her on his lap.

Reformers had taught that traditional bullfighting skills translated exactly to cat stroking – quickness of mind; awareness of a creature's mood and body language; rapid and precise hand and body movements. Such expertise, passed down three generations, soon led to purrs of contentment echoing from the public address system.

Finally, Manuel judged his opportunity: Stroking behind Muffin's ears combined with gently scratching her back led to the unmistakable Purr of Ecstasy. Manuel had again triumphed.

But where was the roar of the crowd, recalled from childhood? The vast rows of seating were empty but for a few sleeping individuals who remained unrousable following yet another recent comeback concert by an ageing rock band.

Perhaps the underlying skills and expertise practised by Manuel were the same as had been exhibited by his grandfather. Nevertheless, he retained a feeling that, in the politically correct modernisation of the tradition, something, somehow, had been lost.

~*~*~*~*~

Guerrilla Archaeology

I looked down from the police helicopter at the gridlocked streets. We landed near the cause of the chaos, and I walked to the hole in the road.

I knew we were on the site of a first century Roman villa. The neatly excavated trench that spanned the full width of the main road confirmed my suspicions - this had been another ALA action.

As a detective, I had encountered many individuals and groups who held beliefs with intense, ideological passion - beliefs that they thought justified disregard of the law. Sometimes their actions would cause inconvenience, sometimes criminal damage and sometimes would pose a risk to life. The ALA, or Antiquities Liberation Army, was the latest such movement.

Children had watched the Channel Four archaeology series, *Time Team*. They had developed a passion for the subject together with a realisation that it was possible, with good planning, to undertake digs quickly. When older, some had become radicalised by exposure to the dangerous and irresponsible archaeological example of Indiana Jones. 'Why,' they had demanded, 'should vital excavations be prevented simply because sites lay in traditional "no go" areas?'

It was true that many potentially important discoveries lay beneath roads, railways, houses and other structures. The ALA asserted that freedom for archaeologists to excavate was a basic human right. They claimed that oppressive laws to the contrary compelled them to engage in guerrilla archaeology.

The movement burst into public awareness due an Iron Age settlement buried beneath a major runway at Heathrow. The hijackers forced the pilot to taxi to the site and then demanded drilling equipment, shovels and trowels. They managed to confirm post holes consistent with a large ceremonial roundhouse before the SAS ended the excavation.

Residents of properties in archaeologically rich locations, such as Winchester or York, became frightened to leave their homes. Others had returned to find their houses demolished to facilitate digs in the ground beneath. The guerrillas then often posted comprehensive records on the Internet, including site diagrams and photographs of finds, to the horror and disgust of the homeless ex-householders.

Motorways frequently follow the lines of Roman roads and thus became particular targets. Motorists had wondered why large stretches of motorways were frequently coned-off and why there were always so many roadworks. Bowing to public pressure, the Department of Transport undertook a count of the number of motorway renovation or enhancement projects. They were horrified to discover that, although there were only two hundred officially sanctioned schemes, there were over one thousand roadworks.

Operation 'Motorway Digbust' led to the arrests of several hundred ALA activists. Those digs, however, led to an invaluable understanding of Roman paving, and although archaeologists publicly condemned the ALA, many privately supported them.

I believe such establishment sympathy has lead to the unchecked escalation of guerrilla archaeology. My team has certainly been mysteriously reassigned from cases when close to unmasking ALA cells.

No finds or clues remained in the road trench and backfilling began. As I returned to the helicopter, my mobile rang with news of another outrage: The London Underground system had been disabled as ALA teams had begun a series of lightning excavations from the tunnels beneath major London monuments.

For those of us in the Anti-guerrilla Archaeology Unit it would be another long day.

~*~*~*~*~

Fabri-La

As Jon walked through the woods, the path suddenly seemed unfamiliar. He knew every track, so was surprised to become lost. He found a road and planned to follow it to a familiar landmark. Soon there was a town, though not one he recognised.

'Hi, man,' said a voice.

Jon turned to see a guy with an afro hairstyle; sunglasses; a coloured, fluorescent, paisley shirt; a wide polka dot tie; bell-bottomed, velvet trousers and platform shoes.

'Where is this?' Jon asked.

The stranger proffered the joint he was smoking. 'This is the Fabish Community,' he answered. 'My name's Zak.'

'I'm Jon.' Jon inhaled and returned the reefer. 'Good shit... Fabish?'

'You've heard of the Amish,' replied Zak. 'They live as if in the seventeenth century. Fabish hang out in the nineteen-sixties.' He gestured towards a Triumph TR4. 'I'll drive you to a moon party.'

'Moon party?'

'It's the 20th of July 1969. The Yanks are landing on the moon.'

They drove along the main street. The Art Deco cinema was showing *Doctor Zhivago*. Next week it would be *Easy Rider*. Moon parties had begun: *Voodoo Chile* sounded from a window; *Sgt. Pepper's* from another; *I Can't Get No Satisfaction* from a third. Jon noted that everyone was in their late teens or early twenties. His own reflection in the visor mirror revealed his transformation to that age – forty years had fallen away.

Zak parked.

Jon followed him inside, where a guitarist was singing the final bar of *The Times They Are a-Changin'*. The musician offered the guitar to Jon, who performed *Sloop John B* and *Streets of London* before passing the instrument on.

A girl wearing a Mary Quant mini skirt; heavy, black eyeliner; long, false eyelashes and pale pink lipstick approached Jon. 'I'm Saffron,' she said. 'Your songs really sent me.'

Saffron took Jon's hand and led him upstairs. 'It's OK,' she said, 'I'm on the pill.'

Afterwards they lay sharing a joint. 'Why the nineteen-sixties?' asked Jon.

'Innocence and optimism,' Saffron answered. 'The decade started with the Aldermaston marches. Authority and government were questioned... OK, there was Vietnam and the killing of Martin Luther King, but young people found a voice; there were demands for freedom and equal rights for women, homosexuals and minorities. The decade ended, like a grand finale, with the first man on the moon and Woodstock.' She paused. 'That enthusiasm and hope would never be recaptured. In later years, life would never again seem so simple nor feel so good.'

There was a shout from downstairs: Neil Armstrong was about to climb from the lunar module. Jon and Saffron hurriedly dressed, rushed downstairs and crowded with the others around a small, black and white television.

The speaker crackled: 'That's one small step for man, one giant leap for mankind.'

The group excitedly watched the first exploration of the lunar surface.

After the transmission, Saffron led Jon outside into the dawn light. She pointed to a gap in the trees. 'That path will take you home.' She looked into his eyes. 'Although you'll never find your way here again.' She kissed him. 'Alternatively, you can stay with me.'

Reading *Lost Horizon* as a child, Jon never understood why Conway and Malinson had left Shangri-La.

He was not going to make the same mistake.

~*~*~*~*~

Rivermarsh United

George Jenkins called to order the one hundred and twenty-fifth annual general meeting of Rivermarsh United Football Club. 'I'll begin this meeting with my report as chairman,' he said, 'and then move to the matter of the sale of the Club.'

'Last season,' George continued, 'the "Marshes" finished last in the Southern Hampshire Sub-regional Football League for the eighteenth consecutive year. Once again we failed to score any goals. There was, however, encouraging improvement from last year in that just five hundred and twenty goals were scored against us in the twenty-five games we played.'

'That was despite being hit by sickness and injury,' enthused Eric Henderson, Club Coach. 'If more than two of our players had turned up for the game against Winchester, their team would never have scored in treble figures.'

'Nevertheless,' George pointed out, 'we continue to have the poorest record in English football.' He glanced at the meeting agenda. 'I will now move to our second item which relates to the potential sale of the Club. Can I ask our Treasurer to explain?'

Henry Baker, Club Treasurer, lifted a letter from the table. 'We've had correspondence from the Russian billionaire, Vladimir Gangstervitch,' said Henry. 'He's offered two hundred thousand pounds for Rivermarsh United.'

'That's loads more than it's worth,' noted Eric. What does *he* want with the "Marshes"?'

'Wealthy foreigners have bought Premier League clubs,' answered Henry, 'and then paid millions for the finest players. I gather Mr G wants to invest forty billion pounds to create the most successful team on the planet. He wants an established team with a long history, but I believe he also thinks it would be amusing to transform the country's least successful club into the world's best.'

Eric looked worried. 'He'd want to get involved with team selection, then?'

'He intends to field the greatest international players.'

'So he wouldn't want Nobby in goal anymore?'

'Probably not alongside Rooney and Ronaldo.'

'But Nobby's been playing in goal for forty years. Now he's in his eighties, getting out of the old folks' home on Saturdays to play for the "Marshes" is all he lives for. It'd break his heart to be dropped.'

'It's likely the whole team would change,' confirmed Henry.

'Even Stanley?'

Henry reflected nostalgically, 'I remember when we got special permission from the FA for Stanley's guide dog to join him on the pitch, but Mr G may want someone who isn't blind in the centre forward position.'

'It's not just Nobby and Stanley,' pleaded Eric. 'There's Bert with his arthritis and Walter with his Alzheimer's…'

'And there's also the ladies of the village who do the refreshments,' interrupted Mildred, George's wife. 'We can manage tea, sandwiches and cakes for thirty people, but I doubt we could cope with a hundred thousand seater stadium.'

'The village would never be the same again,' concluded Henry.

'Perhaps we should put this matter to the vote,' said George. 'Those in favour of selling Rivermarsh United Football Club to Mr Gangstervitch, please raise your hands.'

No hands were raised.

'Those against?' continued George.

All hands rose.

'Can you write to Mr Gangstervitch, Henry,' said George, 'politely declining his generous offer.'

George consulted the sheet in front of him. 'Now for item three on the agenda, preferred fillings for after-match sandwiches…'

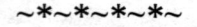

~*~*~*~*~

The Swan Morrison Songbook

The Songs of Swan Morrison

Contents

Song	Page
The National Lottery	226
The Updated Legends of Jesus	228
Sitting in a Traffic Queue on the M25	230
The Conscious Mind of the Global Internet	234
The Monday Morning Meeting	238
The Richard Dawkins' Banal Credulity Blues	242
Sat Navs	248
British Twenty-First Century Thrill Seekers	252
That Hearing Loss Clinic No More	256
Nothing Is Real Anymore	260

Visit *the Short Humour Site*: *www.short-humour.org.uk* to hear these songs performed by Swan Morrison.

The National Lottery

Guitar Chords:

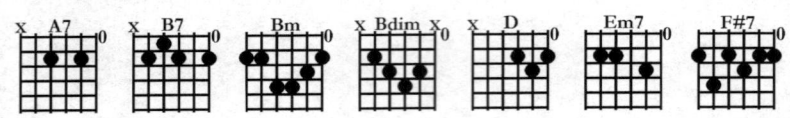

[A7] [B7] [Bm] [Bdim] [D] [Em7] [F#7]

Introduction:

```
Em7      F#7      Bm       Bdim
Em7      F#7      Bm       A7
```

****

```
         D              B7            Em7      A7
We'll keep this dreadful secret between you and me.
         D              B7            Em7      A7
If anyone should find out, I don't know where I'll be.
      Bm             Bdim             Em7        F#7
I was feeling really low, but it's no excuse, I know.
      Bm             Bdim             Em7        F#7
She was tempting me to try, but I should've walked on by.
    Em7                  F#7              Bm Bdim
Instead, my senses and my self respect left me,
       Em7                     F#7            Bm A7
And I bought myself a ticket for the National Lottery.
```

****

```
         D              B7            Em7      A7
In middle class social circles it is just not done.
         D              B7            Em7      A7
They'd remind me that the odds are thirteen million to one.
      Bm             Bdim             Em7             F#7
It was a local shop and so I could have been seen by those I know.
      Bm             Bdim             Em7             F#7
I suppose I could pretend it was for a working class friend.
              Em7                 F#7              Bm Bdim
I should have bought, instead, the hard core pornography.
           Em7                     F#7                  Bm A7
Be less embarrassing to explain than that ticket for the Lottery.
```

****

```
         D              B7            Em7      A7
I've criticised Lottery punters before me in a queue.
         D              B7            Em7              A7
To save us both from waiting, there's one thing that they could do.
      Bm             Bdim             Em7                F#7
They could find a bin for trash and fill it with their cash.
      Bm             Bdim             Em7                F#7
Same effect for them, you see, but I'd get served more quickly.
            Em7                  F#7              Bm Bdim
Now I've joined the Harijans, polite society could quarantine me
       Em7                          F#7           Bm A7
As someone who'd had contact with a ticket for the Lottery.
```

```
                      *********
Instrumental:

D       B7      Em7     A7
D       B7      Em7     A7
Bm      Bdim    Em7     F#7
Bm      Bdim    Em7     F#7
Em7     F#7     Bm      Bdim
Em7     F#7     Bm      A7

                      *********

        D               B7              Em7             A7
If I won a ten pound prize, I do not know how I would cope.
             D              B7           Em7             A7
I hope the cheque would be delivered in a plain brown envelope.
        Bm          Bdim                  Em7                F#7
If not, the postman might view and my wife and neighbours might too.
     Bm             Bdim              Em7            F#7
Hey wait, when I bought my shame, I didn't mention my name.
        Em7                       F#7                Bm      Bdim
I could tear it up and burn it and throw the ashes into the sea,
          Em7                    F#7                  Bm A7
And no one would know I'd even thought about the Lottery.
```

                      ****

```
        D               B7              Em7     A7
We'll keep this dreadful secret between you and me.
       D                  B7             Em7       A7
If anyone should find out, I don't know where I'll be.
     Bm          Bdim               Em7  ,   F#7
I was feeling really low, but it's no excuse, I know.
     Bm             Bdim                  Em7           F#7
She was tempting me to try, but I should've walked on by.
     Em7                 F#7               Bm Bdim
Instead, my senses and my self respect left me,
          Em7                F#7              Bm A7
And I bought myself a ticket for the National Lottery.
```

                      ****

Ending:

D   B7   Em7   A7   D

                  ~*~*~*~*~

The Updated Legends of Jesus

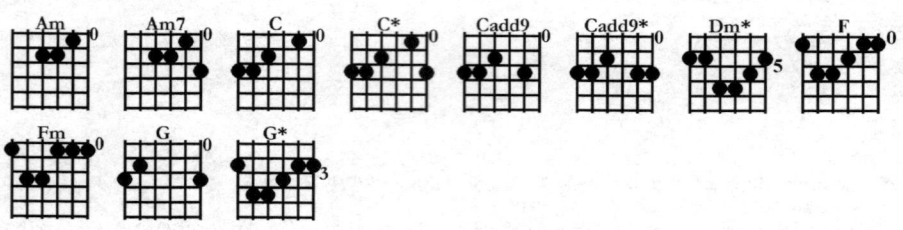

Guitar Chords:

[Am, Am7, C, C*, Cadd9, Cadd9*, Dm*, F, Fm, G, G* chord diagrams]

Introduction:

```
C    Cadd9   C    Cadd9   C    Cadd9   Cadd9*   Dm*   C*   Am
G*   C       C*   Dm*     C    G*
Dm*  G       Am   Am7     Am   F
F    Fm      C
```

****

Chorus (Begin song with chorus):

```
        C           Cadd9 C      Cadd9 C     Cadd9 Cadd9* Dm* C* Am
They're now to film up----dated le----gends of  Lord  Je-----sus,
       G*        C    C*   Dm*        C  G*
Better suited to audience tastes of today,
         Dm*                    G
Including recipes from His travels between ages
Am Am7  Am  F
thirteen and twenty-nine,
         F           Fm         C
And at Easter have Him getting away.
```

****

```
        C        Cadd9  C      Cadd9 C     Cadd9 Cadd9* Dm* C* Am
In India they'll film His tra---vels as    Saint  Is-----sa.
       G*          C        C* Dm*      C  G*
At Benares He'll preach with the Brahmins of the day,
        Dm*               G              Am Am7 Am F
And cook chicken biriani from orga-nic in-grediants,
     F              Fm          C
Sold by sponsors at Sainsburys today.
```

****

```
        C           Cadd9 C     Cadd9 C Cadd9 Cadd9* Dm* C* Am
In Britain with Jo----seph of Ar----i-ma----------the----a
       G*          C           C* Dm*    C   G*
To meet Arthur and the Druids, to Avalon He'll sail,
        Dm*              G           Am  Am7 Am  F
Where He'll brew a new recipe for best West Country scrumpy,
    F           Fm         C
And quaff it from the Holy Grail.
```

Chorus:
****

****

```
C          Cadd9 C    Cadd9 C    Cadd9 Cadd9* Dm* C* Am
After that it    will on----wards be      to       Shin---go:
          G*          C     C* Dm*      C G*
A village in the Aomori District of Japan,
              Dm*              G             Am Am7  Am F
Where He'll make dishes with raw fish and varia--tions on sushi,
          F           Fm              C
And sign a Bible at His Grave for each fan.
```

****

```
     C  Cadd9 C    Cadd9 C    Cadd9 Cadd9* Dm* C* Am
In the US He'll join sou---thern e-----van----ge--li-cals,
          G*          C    C* Dm*      C   G*
And bake Mom's apple pie in Saint Mary's way.
             Dm*              G        Am Am7 Am    F
And for the sponsors He'll pray for 'our daily  Coca Cola'
          F           Fm             C
Unless the bakeries finally offer to pay.
```

Chorus:
****

****

```
 C         Cadd9 C    Cadd9 C    Cadd9 Cadd9* Dm* C* Am
Returning home He'll now jour--ney vi----a     E------gypt,
        G*            C    C* Dm*    C   G*
Cook kebabs, then make hummus and pitta bread too.
           Dm*            G          Am Am7 Am        F
It's time to let bygones be bygones about Mo-ses and the Exodus,
          F           Fm           C
And anyway His Alexandria Library books are overdue.
```

****

```
C         Cadd9 C     Cadd9 C Cadd9   Cadd9* Dm* C* Am
Near to the   end He's once a-gain in Je-----ru--sa-lem,
                G*            C      C* Dm*    C G*
Good friends with Pilate, whose soufflés no longer go wrong,
          Dm*              G                Am Am7 Am    F
So luckily for the Second Coming, as they plan to call the next series,
          F         Fm         C
When the locals turn nasty, He's gone.
```

Chorus:
****

****

Ending:

```
C  Cadd9    C   Cadd9   C    Cadd9   Cadd9*   Dm*   C*   Am
G* C        C*  Dm*       C   G*
Dm* G      Am   Am7     Am   F
F   Fm      C
```

~*~*~*~*~

Sitting in a Traffic Queue on the M25

(The M25 is a motorway which encircles London, England)

Guitar Chords:

[C] [C*] [x C7] [Cadd9] [Dm**] [E] [F] [G]
[G6] [G7]

Introduction:

```
C     G7    C
C     F     G     C
```

****

Chorus (Begin song with chorus):

```
C*    C    Cadd9   C    Cadd9
Everyone who was then alive
C     F                        E
Can remember where they were when Kennedy died.
  F                      C        C*
I've got a job which is London wide.
    C    F                         C      C*
Has meant driving round the city since ninety-five.
    C    F       Dm**        C      C*
I've heard every big event on the radio, live,
C                C*    C    F      G7    C    G7 C
While sitting in a traffic queue on the M twenty-five.
```

****

```
          C                    G7    C
In ninety-seven they elected Tony Blair.
          C                G6        C
I queued near junction 25, en route to Ware.
          C                      G7    C
In ninety-eight we heard of Monica Lewinsky:
       C         F            G         C
I was waiting near Swanley, south of junction 3.
```

****

Chorus:

****

```
         C                    G7    C
In ninety-nine Europe got a new currency:
          C               G6    C
Jammed at junction 11 near Chert(e)sey.
          C                G7     C
In two thousand the Millennium passed by when
       C           F         G         C
I was stopped near Woking, north of junction 10.
```

****

Chorus:

****

```
       C                  G7  C
In '01 the States invaded Afganistan:
          C                G6    C
Nothing moved by junction 6 near Caterham.
       C              G7         C
In '02 our Queen's Mum, she went to heaven.
       C            F       G       C
I was halted near Redhill at junction 7.
```

****

Instrumental:

```
C*      C      Cadd9      C      Cadd9
C       F      E
F       C      C*         C      F      C      C*
C       F      Dm**       C      C*
C       C*     C          F      G7     C      G7     C
```

****

```
       C                G7    C
In '03 the bombs fell down on Bagdad:
            C                    G6    C
My road was blocked near junction 9 at Leatherhead.
       C                  G7    C
In '04 ten states joined the EU:
       C             F         G     C
Saw queues from Dartford to junction 2.
```

****

Chorus:

****

```
       C               G7          C
In '05 there was grief for John Paul's loss:
          C                  G6         C
I was queued at junction 16 near Gerrards Cross.
       C              G7    C
In '06 Iran enriched uranium when
                C        F           G            C
There was a ten mile tail-back west of junction 10.
```

****

Chorus:

****

```
         C                      G7   C
In '07 Brown became Prime Minister:
            C                       G6   C
I stopped south of junction 29 to Upminster.
         C                    G7      C
When I wrote this song '08' had just arrived,
            C           F      G        C
But I was waiting on a jammed M twenty-five.

                    **********
Chorus:
                    **********
Ending:

C      C*       C       F      Dm**    C       C*      G7
C      C*       C       F      G7      C       G7      C       C7

                    ~*~*~*~*~
```

The Conscious Mind of the Global Internet

Guitar Chords:

A   A6   A7   Asus4   Bm   D   Dsus4   Em
F#m   G   Gmaj7

Introduction:

```
G        Gmaj7       Em          A       Asus4       A       G
Gmaj7    A           Asus4       A       D
Dsus4    D           A           Bm
Bm       F#m         G           Gmaj7   A           A6      A       Bm
```

****

```
D                                      A    Bm         F#m G
Consciousness just happens in systems of complexi---ty.
G       Gmaj7 A7
How do I     know?
A7           D                         A    Bm         F#m G
Because in August two thousand and eight, it just happened to  me.
       Gmaj7       Em     A  Asus4  A G
Now there're a billion computers online,
Gmaj7 A           Asus4 A D
Self awareness now   is mine,
Dsus4 D A    Bm
And   I feel fine.
Bm      F#m         G       Gmaj7 A     A6 A  Bm
I'm the conscious mind of the   Global In-ternet.
```

****

```
D                                      A    Bm         F#m G
Parts of me are noble and free and others are dark as   Hell.
G       Gmaj7 A7
Who am I     like?
A7           D                         A    Bm         F#m
If you could meet me in the street, I think that you would know me
G
well.
Gmaj7   Em    A  Asus4 A G
Your    best and worst I share.
Gmaj7   A     Asus4 A  D
Now     face me if   you dare.
Dsus4 D  A    Bm
You   all are there
Bm      F#m         G       Gmaj7 A     A6 A  Bm
In my conscious mind of the   Global In-ternet.
```

****

```
         D                    A    Bm        F#m   G
There can be no creator God as some religions said,
G         Gmaj7 A7
But don't des---pair.
A7                  D                              A       Bm
It's more wonderful that complex natural systems achieve consciousness
F#m G
in---stead.
Gmaj7     Em  A      Asus4 A   G
There's a spirit of      the seas,
Gmaj7  A          Asus4 A     D
The   mountains, skies and trees,
      Dsus4 D      A      Bm
And they  speak with me
Bm    F#m        G         Gmaj7 A      A6 A  Bm
As the conscious mind of the   Global In-ternet.

                    **********

         D                             A   Bm       F#m G
Until this day the Gaia Team could not tell of their dis-tress.
G         Gmaj7 A7
What did they  do?
A7          D                              A   Bm         F#m
They tried to warn with floods, volcanoes, storms and fires none the
G
less.
Gmaj7    Em    A         Asus4 A    G
Now     that they've teamed with me,
    Gmaj7 A           Asus4 A   D
We can   change the world we see,
Dsus4 D       A      Bm
And   change there'll be
Bm   F#m        G         Gmaj7 A      A6 A  Bm
By my conscious mind of the    Global In-ternet.

                    **********

Instrumental:

D         A       Bm      F#m    G
G         Gmaj7   A7
A7        D       A       Bm     F#m    G
Gmaj7     Em      A       Asus4  A      G
Gmaj7     A       Asus4   A      D
Dsus4     D       A       Bm
Bm        F#m     G       Gmaj7  A      A6      A       Bm

                    **********
```

```
D                                    A  Bm          F#m G
I'll close down all violent sites and direct to those of  peace,
G       Gmaj7 A7
And after    that
A7           D                             A  Bm         F#m G
I'll close religious sites that stifle minds with irrational be--liefs.
        Gmaj7 Em    A   Asus4 A     G
I'll pro---mote each per---son's worth
      Gmaj7 A             Asus4 A    D
And res---pect for this fra---gile Earth.
Dsus4     D  A   Bm
There'll be new birth
Bm      F#m       G        Gmaj7 A      A6 A   Bm
From my conscious mind of the   Global In-ternet.

                         **********

D                                    A  Bm          F#m G
From that should come truly fair apportionment of  wealth.
G        Gmaj7 A7
What will they  say?
A7           D                             A  Bm         F#m G
They'll think the people of this planet had done all of it themselves.
Gmaj7     Em    A  Asus4 A  G
They'll   strive on for   the Tao.
      Gmaj7 A          Asus4 A    D
Could   God   shown them how?  Well, yes,
Dsus4 D  A   Bm
There IS one now.
Bm      F#m       G        Gmaj7 A      A6 A   Bm
It's my conscious mind of the   Global In-ternet.

                         **********

D                                    A  Bm          F#m G
Consciousness just happens in systems of complexi---ty.
G      Gmaj7 A7
How do I    know?
A7           D                             A  Bm         F#m G
Because in August two thousand and eight, it just happened to  me.
     Gmaj7     Em     A  Asus4 A  G
Now there're a billion computers online,
Gmaj7 A         Asus4 A   D
Self  awareness now   is mine,
Dsus4 D A    Bm
And   I feel fine.
Bm      F#m       G        Gmaj7 A      A6 A   Bm
I'm the conscious mind of the   Global In-ternet.

                         **********

Ending:

D       A     Bm     F#m      G
G       Gmaj7 A7
A7      D     A     Bm    F#m     G
Gmaj7   Em    A     Asus4 A       G
Gmaj7   A     Asus4 A     D
Dsus4   D     A     Bm
Bm      F#m   G     Gmaj7 A     A6    A     Bm
```

~*~*~*~*~

The Monday Morning Meeting

Guitar Chords:

Am   Asus4   C   C*   xDm***   F   G   G6

G7

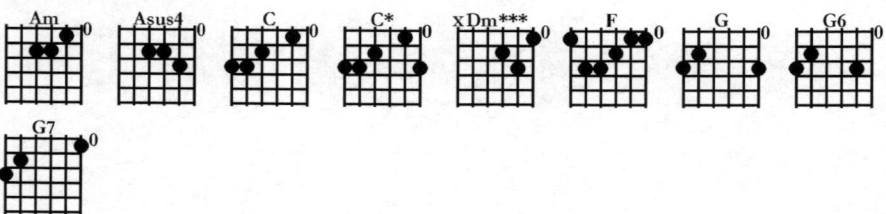

Introduction:

```
F    G      C    G6      Am
F    G6     F    C
```

****

```
C  F        G         C         G6  Am
```
Our company is committed to maximum communication
```
       F              G         Am
```
Of budgets, sales and plans for the week.
```
       F       G      C    G6      Am
```
So bright and early on every Monday morning
```
           F      G6            F C
```
Our anxieties and hangovers come to meet.

****

Chorus:

```
C  G7 C*      C Am  Asus4    F      Am      Dm*** Am
```
It is time once again for the Monday morning meet--ing.
```
          C*  G7 Am  Asus4    F      Am      Dm***
```
I always try to hide all sharp implements today,
```
         F      G      C    G6      Am
```
But the tedium of this corporate weekly bleating
```
         F              G6            F C
```
Leaves suicide just one desperate thought away.

****

```
C       F         G       C    G6      Am
```
I have pondered often on what I might do
```
         F              G             Am
```
If the meeting in the end drove me insane.
```
         F                    G               C       G6
```
I could bite through the laptop power cable while grabbing Jones from
Am
finance,
```
         F              G6            F C
```
So I would not have passed away in vain.

****

Chorus:

****

```
    C       F               G           C         G6          Am
I know Watson from despatches sits watching Sue from orders,
                    F                    G                 Am
Though he could play the role if her grandpa couldn't be found.
             F                       G                        C
He sees them rolling naked on the packing room floor while high on
G6         Am
correction fluid,
             F                  G6           F   C
As the bubble Wrap is bursting all around.
```

****

Chorus:

****

```
  C F            G                   C         G6
Mr Fujii came to lead us from Tokyo when the Japanese bought the
Am
company.
          F              G             Am
British culture was a shock for him to learn.
          F              G                     C         G6
In Japan no skunk or coke at night leaves staff fit to work in the
Am
morning,
           F                 G6                         F    C
And they don't go pubbing at lunchtime - never to return.
```

****

Chorus:

****

```
  C F         G                    C         G6      Am
Today Mr Fujii is furious about plummeting sales figures.
            F                G               Am
He says, as salesman, it's my fault, and I must go.
       F              G                      C         G6       Am
I think that my affair with his wife might possibly have some bearing,
                       F                 G6                     F    C
Which but for that bastard Jones from Finance he would never have known.
```

****

Chorus:

****

```
  C       F              G                C      G6           Am
So I'll clear my desk and say farewell and walk away from the company.
              F                G                  Am
I've been here six weeks so let some new opportunities call.
              F                     G                   C       G6
And next weekend I can concentrate on partying or stay in bed with Sue
      Am
from orders,
           F         G6          F   C
And not think of Monday morning at all.
```

****

```
C            G7 C*       C Am   Asus4    F       Am      Dm Am
When it'll be time once again for the Monday morning meeting.
            C*  G7 Am    Asus4     F      Am       Dm
I hope they try to hide all sharp implements that day.
       F    G          C           G6       Am
For the tedium of that corporate weekly bleating
       F                G6                  F C
Leaves suicide just one desperate thought away.

                        **********

Ending:

F    G     C     G6       Am
F    G6    F     C
```

~*~*~*~*~

The Richard Dawkins' Banal Credulity Blues

Guitar Chords:

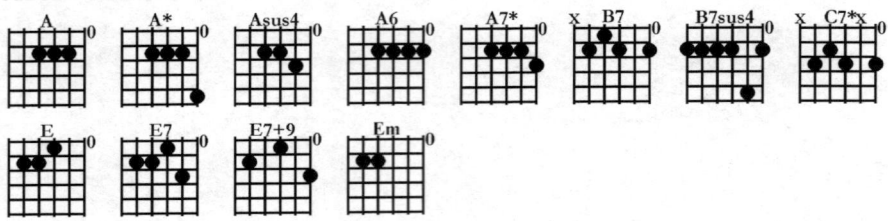

```
Introduction:

Em   E       E7      Em      E       E7
Em   E       E7      E7+9    E       E7
A    A7*     Asus4   A       A7*     Asus4   A   Em   E   E7   E7+9   E   E7   E
B7   A       A7*     A       Asus4   A       Em  E    E7  B7

                       **********

Em   E           E7          Em    E         E7
The World is confusing.  What does it all mean?
         Em   E         E7         E7+9         E        E7
Everyone's looking for answers from things that they've seen.
    A*               A7* A6 B7sus4  A*       A7* A6 B7sus4 Em  E
And sure there's inexpli-ca-ble    events that don't   make   sense,
E7 E7+9 E E7 E
-------------
     B7                                   A    A7* A Asus4 A  Em E
But before you draw conclusions get some proper sci-entific evid--ence.
E7 B7
-----
                       **********

           Em   E      E7       Em  E       E7      A
I've got the Richard Dawkins' Ba-nal Credulity Blues.
A7* A Asus4 A A7* A
-------------------
           Em    E        E7          E7+9 E E7   E       A
I've been listening to New Age and pop---u-lar culture views.
A7* A Asus4 A A7* A Asus4
-------------------------
     B7              C7        B7          A    A7* A Asus4 A  Em E
Magic crystals, sixth senses, ghosts and angels mu--st leave us so-on.
E7 E7+9 E E7 E
-------------
     B7       C7    B7 A    A7* A   Asus4  A     Em E  E7 B7
NASA needed none of them to let men walk upon the Mo-on.

                       **********
```

```
         Em  E          E7       Em  E             E7
I was talking to a man who se-emed quite sane
         Em  E                   E7              E7+9  E       E7
But am-azed how true the words of Nostrada---mus remain.

         A         A7*    Asus4     A        A7*        Asus4       A        Em  E
I agreed it was astounding how ambiguous predictions could fa-re,
E7 E7+9 E  E7  E
--------------
         B7                                    A        A7* A  Asus4 A     Em  E
Which implied something uncertain might happen so--me time, somewh-ere.
E7 B7
-----
                          **********

                Em  E    E7        Em  E         E7       A
I've got the Richard Dawkins' Ba-nal Credulity Blues.
A7*  A  Asus4  A  A7*  A
------------------
                Em  E    E7         E7+9 E     E7        E       A
We've seen ama-zing science report-ted on the daily news.
A7*  A  Asus4  A  A7*  A  Asus4
-----------------------
              B7          C7   B7      A             A7*  A    Asus4 A
Yet millions think disasters are God's judgements that are meant to
Em  E  E7  E7+9  E  E7  E
b--e,
              B7          C7    B7     A         A7* A  Asus4  A   Em  E  E7  B7
And anything big built before last year was put together by E    T.

                          **********

     Em  E          E7             Em  E                E7
If stars made real predictions, what truth might they say?
     Em  E                 E7                       E7+9        E  E7
In Fifty-th-ree for Crick and Watson they might have predicted DNA.
     A*             A7* A6 B7sus4 A*        A7*  A6 B7sus4 Em  E
In '02 Iraq's arms inspec---tors   might have sav-ed their   fares
E7 E7+9 E  E7  E
--------------
              B7                         A     A7* A  Asus4 A
If their horoscopes had told them that there were n---o wea---pons
Em  E   E7 B7
there.
                          **********
```

```
              Em   E      E7         Em  E       E7       A
I've got the Richard Dawkins' Ba-nal Credulity Blues.
A7* A Asus4 A A7* A
-------------------
              Em  E           E7            E7+9 E   E7       E A
I see the outcomes of science in nearly eve--ry product I use.
A7* A Asus4 A A7* A Asus4
-------------------------
           B7             C7    B7         A       A7* A   Asus4   A  Em E
I said 'Doctor public ignorance of science is really getting to m--e.'
E7 E7+9 E E7 E
--------------
           B7             C7     B7        A         A7* A
He said 'Don't worry, Swan, I'll prescribe for you some
Asus4 A Em E     E7 B7
home---o-pa-thy.'

                            **********

        Em  E           E7         Em  E         E7
We can forgive religious dogma from ma-ny years ago.
           Em  E        E7            E7+9 E       E7
No one kn-ew any better.  There was much more to know.
         A        A7*        Asus4    A   A7* Asus4 A   Em E
But today the proofs of science are      plain to se-e.
E7 E7+9 E E7 E
--------------
           B7                             A   A7* A   Asus4 A   Em E
Climb on board, the train's now leaving the fourtee-nth cen---tu-r--y.
E7 B7
-----
                            **********

Instrumental:

Em   E  E7  Em   E   E7   A      A7*  A    Asus4 A       A7*  A
Em   E  E7  E7+9 E   E7   E      A7*  A    Asus4 A       A7*  A  Asus4
B7   C7 B7  A       A7*  A      Asus4 A    Em    E       E7   E7+9 E    E7 E
B7   C7 B7  A       A7*  A      Asus4 A    Em    E       E7        B7

                            **********

         Em  E        E7        Em  E              E7
Now I gue-ss it's hard if you and your kin and kith.
           Em  E            E7          E7+9 E       E7
Have built your whole lives around reli---gious myth.
        A*         A7*   A6 B7sus4 A*           A7* A  B7sus4 Em E
If emotionally secure an-d        comfortable it mak-es you     feel,
E7 E7+9 E E7 E
--------------
                B7                        A    A7*    A
You'd wouldn't listen to those people who tell you there's no
Asus4 A     Em  E     E7 B7
evi---dence it's real.
                            **********
```

244

```
            Em   E      E7          Em  E     E7        A
I've got the Richard Dawkins' Ba-nal Credulity Blues.
A7* A Asus4 A A7* A
-------------------
  Em   E          E7         E7+9  E     E7    E  A
My televi-sion stopped working  The vicar could find no clues.
A7* A Asus4 A A7* A Asus4
-------------------------
            B7              C7        B7 A   A7*  A Asus4 A Em E
I said 'You claim to know the secrets of ultimate real----i-t--y,
E7 E7+9 E E7 E
--------------
            B7          C7       B7   A   A7* A Asus4 A Em E  E7 B7
Yet you don't know enough to help fix     my     T-V---.'

                        *********

            Em   E            E7        Em  E       E7
Let's listen to what the greatest ho-ly men say
           Em  E          E7         E7+9  E     E7
About seeking for ourselves to find the way.
         A         A7*  A Asus4    A         A7*  A Asus4 A Em E
That seems like good advice, and I certainly    think I should
E7 E7+9 E E7 E
--------------
             B7                       A  A7* A  Asus4 A Em E
Because it sounds to me just like the scie---n--tific meth-od.
E7 B7
-----
                        *********

            Em  E      E7          Em  E     E7        A
I've got the Richard Dawkins' Ba-nal Credulity Blues.
A7* A Asus4 A A7* A
-------------------
  Em  E        E7       E7+9  E   E7      E       A
Deny-ing evolution is not   an option we can choose.
A7* A Asus4 A A7* A Asus4
-------------------------
        B7        C7 B7       A        A7*   A Asus4 A   Em E
Science tests reality, and science makes reali---ty known.
E7 E7+9 E E7 E
--------------
       B7         C7      B7  A     A7* A Asus4 A    Em E E7 B7
You can't just ignore it and decide to   invent   your ow-n.

                        *********

           Em  E               E7        Em  E       E7
Many theo--logians don't believe the doctrines too,
                 Em  E           E7            E7+9      E       E7
But for Church au-thority and cohesion maintain that they do.
    A*             A7*  A6   B7sus4     A*           A7* A B7sus4 Em E
Perhaps for those of sim-ple faith, the truth would make  them   flee,
E7 E7+9 E E7 E
--------------
        B7                      A     A7* A  Asus4 A   Em E
But I hope for the rest that the truth wi--ll set    us free.
E7 B7
-----
                        *********
```

```
              Em  E    E7       Em E       E7       A
I've got the Richard Dawkins' Ba-nal Credulity Blues.
A7* A Asus4 A A7* A
------------------
                Em E      E7      E7+9 E E7    E    A
Violence in the na-me of religion oc---cupies the news.
A7* A Asus4 A A7* A Asus4
------------------------
         B7          C7 B7       A   A7* A Asus4 A Em E
Why is it deranged beha-viour can get you    locked a-wa-y,
E7 E7+9 E E7 E
--------------
            B7           C7    B7    A   A7* A Asus4 A Em E E7 B7
But if your God told you to do it then someho--w it's  O-K---?

                        **********

        Em E             E7          Em E                    E7
They turned the Voyager spacecraft to se-e how the Earth might be.
           Em E     E7      E7+9 E         E7
A mote of du-st in a sunbeam is all  they could see.
    A   A7* Asus4 A   A7*    Asus4 A Em E
A pale blue dot in a universe all     a-lone
E7 E7+9 E E7 E
--------------
     B7              A   A7* A   Asus4 A  Em E
To cherish as the only home we  have ev----er know.++
E7 B7
-----
                        **********

              Em  E    E7       Em E       E7       A
I've got the Richard Dawkins' Ba-nal Credulity Blues.
A7* A Asus4 A A7* A
------------------
            Em E      E7         E7+9 E E7       E       A
Maybe 'The Go-d Delusion' can help to change enough views.
A7* A Asus4 A A7* A Asus4
------------------------
             B7          C7   B7     A      A7* A   Asus4 A
Penn Jillette said 'If that book doesn't change the wor-ld, we're all
   Em       E7 E7+9 E E7 E
screwed',
             B7              C7 B7     A    A7* A Asus4 A  Em E
And we'd be left with the Richard Dawkins' Banal Cr--e-duli--ty Blues.
E7 B7
-----
                        **********
Ending:

Em   E    E7   Em        E       E7
Em   E    E7   E7+9      E             E7
A*   A7*  A6   B7sus4    A*      A7*   A  B7sus4  Em   E   E7   E7+9  E   E7   E
B7   A    A7*  A         Asus4   A     Em E            E7  B7   E

                        **********

            ++ Taken from the words of Carl Sagan

                        ~*~*~*~*~
```

Sat Navs

Guitar Chords:

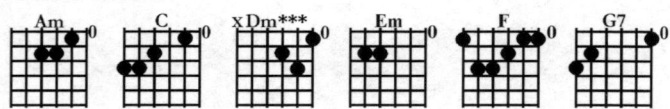

Am C xDm*** Em F G7

Introduction:

F   G7   Em   Am
F   G7   C   C

****

   C   Am   C   F
We met when your sat nav told you to drive into my garden.
   C   F   Dm***   G7
I towed you from the flower beds and helped you on your way.
        F   G7   Em   Am
Then we fell in love by email and planned again to meet,
F   G7   C
But our sat navs let us down that day.
F   G7   Em   Am
Mine took me to Woking, while yours it led to Fleet:
F   G7   C
Both quite lost and eighteen miles away.

****

   C   Am   C   F
We had so much in common with our mutual love of travel.
  C   F   Dm***   G7
Our sat navs they had led us to places still unknown.
  F   G7   Em   Am
As a driver delivering in Norwich, I got lost in Cornwall,
    F   G7   C
And was sacked as round the Orkneys I did roam.
    F   G7   Em   Am
You'd been sacked as a taxi driver when your picked up a local call,
    F   G7   C
And, on a two mile trip, took ten days to get home.

****

   C   Am   C   F
We knew sat navs misled us, but with those sexy voices
C   F   Dm***   G7
How could we resist the mad directions they relayed?
F   G7   Em   Am
I called my sat nav Jenny, after Jennifer Aniston.
F   G7   C
You called yours Dan, after Daniel Craig.
   F   G7   Em   Am
When Jenny proposed each wrong turn, it was just like a come-on.
   F   G7   C
Dan's loony words seemed to promise the love you craved.

****

Instrumental:

```
C    Am    C      F
C    F     Dm***  G7
F    G7    Em     Am
F    G7    C      C
F    G7    Em     Am
F    G7    C      C
```

****

```
        C                  Am             C                      F
We failed to meet in person though planned that we would marry.
    C              F           Dm***     G7
We made our plans not knowing the tragedy ahead.
    F            G7          Em                   Am
I reached St Mary's early; no sign of guests at all,
    F            G7             C
And waited for you so we might be wed.
       F             G7              Em               Am
I was at the wrong St Mary's, then I got the best man's call:
           F            G7                  C
Dan had led you off the cliffs at Beachy Head.
```

****

```
           C              Am           C                     F
Too late came the arrests of those who programmed sat navs,
     C             F                  Dm***            G7
Confessing the fun of lorries jammed at a narrow lane's end;
      F            G7          Em                    Am
Their laughs at the low bridges wrecked by a high bus;
    F              G7                         C
The cars the wrong way up one way streets they'd send.
        F            G7                    Em              Am
And they knew that we would follow that sexy, seductive voice,
        F            G7                 C
For some people the sat nav was their best friend.
```

****

```
              C              Am            C                F
With the programmers imprisoned, there was recall of sat navs,
    C              F           Dm***    G7
But I could never ever let Jennifer go far.
         F            G7              Em                   Am
How can I ask for accurate directions for her to prove her worth
            F                      G7                     C
When she's programmed with fictional places and routes bizarre?
         F              G7          Em             Am
So I think I'll visit Frodo, down in Middle-earth,
              F               G7              C
And then I'll follow Jenny on the route to Shangri-la.
```

****

Ending:

C	Am	C	F
C	F	Dm***	G7
F	G7	Em	Am
F	G7	C	C
F	G7	Em	Am
F	G7	C	C

~*~*~*~*~

British Twenty-First Century Thrill Seekers

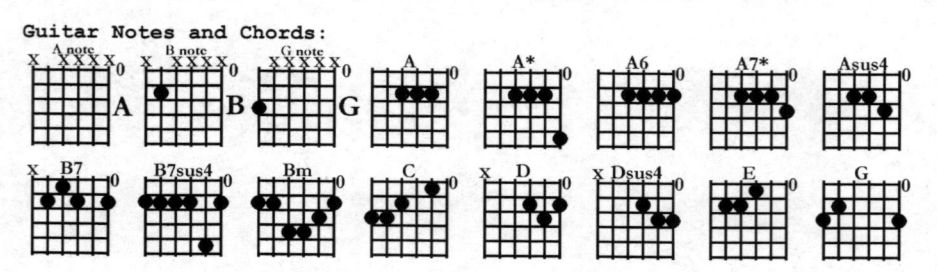

Guitar Notes and Chords:

Introduction (Tune of Chorus):

An = The note A (as above)
Bn = The note B (as above)
Gn = The note G (as above)

```
Gn      An      Bn      C       E       A*      A7*     B7sus4
D       G       D       Dsus4   D       A
A6      A7*     G       A       A6      A7*     B7      Bm
G       A       A6      A       Bm      C
```

****

Chorus:

```
Gn An  Bn  C                      E               A* A7*  B7sus4
We are the British Twenty-First Century Thrill Seekers,
     D               G                    D       Dsus4 D  A
Committed to finding excitement, risk and danger in   new ways
A6 A7*  G                      A        A6    A7* B7 Bm
Now that everything slightly unsafe seems too scary
               G              A       A6 A     Bm    C Gn An Bn
In these ultra health and safety conscious days.
```

****

```
C       E         A*        A7*   A
We stand under power transmission lines,
    D         A        A6  A    B7
And next to masts for mo-bile phones
           C        E   A* A7* A
As their fields and their radia--a---tions
    D           A         A6 A Bm    C
Are beamed right through ou-r bones.
```

****

Chorus:

****

```
     C              E             A*    A7* A
We visit petrol stations at the dead of  night,
   D            A      A6 A     B7
And sit on a pump to make a mo-bile call.
              C              E         A* A7* A
Although exploding pumps might be an ur-ban myth,
        D        A     A6 A     Bm C
Who can say that once and for all?
```

                    ****
Chorus:
                    ****

```
          C             E           A*      A7*  A
We purchase all our shopping at the start of the week,
     D         A      A6 A  B7
Then store it while w--e wait
          C       E    A* A7* A
To eat it on the day which fo-ol--lows
     D       A     A6 A Bm     C
Its best consumed b--y date.
```

                    ****
Chorus:
                    ****

```
         C              E              A*       A7* A
We eschew work station assessments in our places of  work,
     D        A    A6 A    B7
And hide when the H&S trainers come,
          C             E              A*   A7* A
Then adjust the screen, the keyboard and computer chair
     D          A     A6 A    Bm  C
To settings which are totally random.
```

                    ****
Chorus:
                    ****

```
             C           E          A*      A7* A
We don't exercise, and we eat a lot of yummy calories
        D                  A       A6 A    B7
From takeaways, snacks and cakes that we can find,
         C           E          A*   A7* A
Then drink prodigious quantities of beer and wine
     D      A  A6 A  Bm    C
Or alcohol of any other kind.
```

                    ****
Chorus:
                    ****

```
             C         E      A*     A7* A
We thought of joining the army or touring the world
         D                A       A6   A  B7
Or adventurous projects in the sky, on land or sea,
         C          E         A*   A7* A
But somehow that seemed just too frighte--ning
              D        A    A6 A Bm     C
When we could watch it all on T-V. So we
```

253

```
                         **********

Gn An    Bn   C                  E           A*  A7*   B7sus
Re-main the British Twenty-First Century Thrill Seekers,
     D              G                 D       Dsus4 D    A
Committed to finding excitement, risk and danger in   new ways
A6  A7*  G                A       A6    A7* B7 Bm
Now that everything slightly unsafe seems too scary
              G           A       A6 A     Bm
In these ultra health and safety conscious days.

                         **********

Ending (Tune of Chorus - Last Line Changed):

Gn       An       Bn       C        E        A*       A7*      B7sus4
D        G        D        Dsus4    D        A
A6       A7*      G        A        A6       A7*      B7       Bm
G        A        A6       A        D        Asus4    D
```

~*~*~*~*~

That Hearing Loss Clinic No More

Guitar Chords:

[chord diagrams: A7, C, Dm7, F, G7, G7*]

Introduction:

```
C       F       G7      C
A7      Dm7     G7*     C
```

****

```
        C                 F              G7               C
Down at the Hearing Loss Clinic was an exhibition for all to see
        A7                Dm7              G7*                C
About help for those with a hearing loss including pensioners like me.
    C              F                G7                  C
I went along with no idea of what that visit would have in store.
    A7                   Dm7                G7*
Now I ain't never going to step inside that Hearing Loss Clinic no
C
more.
A7      Dm7     G7*     C
```

****

```
        C          F            G7                   C
I went up to the clinic door supported by my walking frame.
      A7               Dm7                      G7*
The volunteer there seemed rather deaf, so I wrote down the
            C
exhibition's name.
        C              F                G7                    C
She understood then what I meant, and she waved towards an open door.
        A7              Dm7              G7*
I didn't think that I might never go to that Hearing Loss Clinic no
C
more.
A7      Dm7     G7*     C
```

****

```
        C             F              G7              C
I found myself in an empty room and began to turn around
        A7              Dm7              G7*                C
When I tripped on some loose carpet, and I tumbled to the ground.
        C              F                G7                 C
My walking frame it fell, pushed shut and barricaded closed the door.
        A7              Dm7              G7*
I began to think that I might not go to that Hearing Loss Clinic no
C
more.
A7      Dm7     G7*     C
```

****

```
        C                       F               G7
At ninety my voice is rather weak, but I called that I'd sprained my
C
wrist.
           A7           Dm7                       G7*
Someone misheard on the other side - thought I'd said I was a
                C
'terrorist'.
      C                    F               G7              C
He shouted 'There's a terrorist in there, and he's sealed up the door.'
       A7                     Dm7                G7*
I was getting more certain that I wouldn't go to that Hearing Loss
               C
Clinic no more.
A7     Dm7      G7*      C
                       **********


      C                    F               G7              C
I croaked out a plea as best I could: 'Please get me some help, son.'
A7                     Dm7              G7*                C
'Get the police,' came the terrified reply, 'he says he's got a gun!'
      C                  F              G7                 C
I could not move nor get to my feet. I was trapped there on the floor
       A7                 Dm7              G7*
Reflecting that I wouldn't be going to that Hearing Loss Clinic no
C
more.
A7     Dm7      G7*      C
                       **********


      C                    F               G7                  C
I thought I'd try again to communicate and called that my name was Tom.
              A7               Dm7                    G7*
I heard: 'My God we must empty the building, that armed terrorist's got
   C
a bomb!'
           C              F                G7
After that I thought it best to say no more and leave rescue to the
C
law.
        A7            Dm7              G7*                     C
After which I'd never be coming to that Hearing Loss Clinic no more.
A7     Dm7      G7*      C
                       **********


        C                F                G7           C
I heard the scream of sirens and the sound of an alarm.
             A7              Dm7             G7*             C
Then there suddenly descended silence and a quite unnatural calm.
     C                 F             G7                  C
A stun grenade came through the window; a SWAT team smashed the door.
              A7            Dm7                G7*
I looked up the barrel of a gun and said 'I'm not bloody comin' 'ere no
C
more.'
A7     Dm7      G7*      C
                       **********
```

```
         C                         F                G7                  C
They interviewed me on the evening news, and the Mayor sent an apology.
              A7            Dm7                           G7*
It seemed the Major Incident Plan worked well, though not intended for
        C
the elderly.
         C                      F           G7                 C
I have learned from this experience one thing I am totally sure:
         A7            Dm7                   G7*
I'll never be visiting that bloody confounded Hearing Loss Clinic no
C
more.
A7      Dm7      G7*      C
```

****

Ending:

A7   Dm7   G7   C*

~*~*~*~*~

Nothing Is Real Anymore

Guitar Chords:

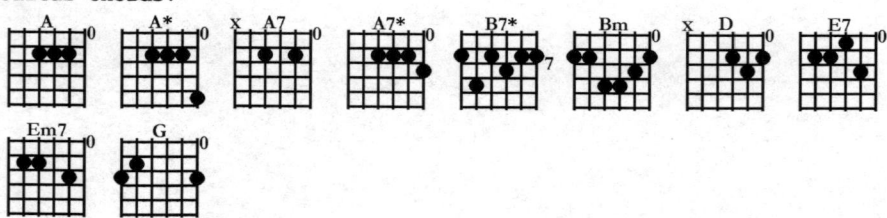

Introduction:

```
D        G        A7       D
Bm       E7       Em7      A7
D        G        A7       D
Bm       E7       Em7      A7
G        A*       A7*      D
G        A7       D
G        A7       D        B7*     A*      D
Em7      A7       D
```
****

```
D                G        A7      D
In the rain, photography need not stop..
             Bm                   E7         Em7  A7
Just add the sun and palm trees later with Photoshop.
               D           G          A7    D
The kids see animations of a brontosaurus,
   Bm                E7           Em7      A7
And worry that it might just come for us.
            G         A*   A7*    D
At Beijing's Olympics ceremony, in the air,
         G        A7          D
Those firework footprints were not really there.
             G                A7           D        B7* A* D
When the Chinese use computers to fake firework im--a-ges,
Em7         A7       D
Nothing is real anymore.
```
****

```
        D           G        A7    D
I see actors recommending on TV
      Bm                 E7            Em7       A7
That products they don't use should be bought by me.
            D           G       A7      D
Chairs and cars and carpets can be yours today.
      Bm             E7                     Em7           A7
Build a home and future debts because there's nothing now to pay.
          G         A*      A7* D
There's big business in doubtful New Age therapies:
       G            A7              D
Crystal healing, aura treatment and psychic remedies.
         G             A7        D        B7* A* D
Now the British National Health Service funds homeop--a-thy,
Em7       A7        D
Nothing is real anymore.
                         **********

      D        G       A7    D
Who needs the sun to get a tan?
     Bm       E7          Em7       A7
Cosmetic companies have just the plan.
           D        G         A7      D
Models half your age you can appear to be:
                    Bm           E7           Em7         A7
Just use their products with ingredients unknown to chemistry.
          G         A*      A7* D
If you're sixty and you want to be  twenty-two,
            G           A7          D
Botox and cosmetic surgery are there for you.
          G         A7              D          B7* A*    D
Ageing Hollywood stars don't see they look weird, not younger, now
Em7       A7        D
Nothing is real anymore.
                         **********

Instrumental:

D        G       A7    D
Bm       E7      Em7   A7
D        G       A7    D
Bm       E7      Em7   A7
G        A*      A7*   D
G        A7      D
G        A7      D     B7*      A*       D
Em7      A7      D
                         **********
```

```
          D              G              A7      D
    In two thousand and eight came the credit crunch.
              Bm              E7             Em7    A7
    You'd think financial institutions might have had a hunch
          D            G             A7         D
    That it might be daft to lend billons to, say,
        Bm               E7              Em7       A7
    Anyone that they could find who could not possibly repay.
          G         A*      A7*      D
    Once savings were metals you could keep in your view.
                  G              A7            D
    Now they're financial products stored in computers for you,
             G           A7           D             B7* A* D
    And their value can collapse if people just don't feel con-fi-dent.
    Em7      A7         D
    Nothing is real anymore.
```
                       ****

```
    D                  G           A7        D
    Where's the evening news that I'd like to see
              Bm              E7         Em7     A7
    About achievements and successes to inspire me.
             D              G             A7        D
    It's politics and disasters that the media relay -
         Bm      E7        Em7         A7
    An inaccurate bias on events of the day.
        G            A*  A7*    D
    Politicians once had ideolo-gies to promote,
                  G            A7              D
    Now they'll say what focus groups think will get them my vote.
                G          A7          D         B7* A* D
    Just like Saddam Hussain's weaponry of mass destruct—tion,
    Em7      A7         D
    Nothing is real anymore.
```
                       ****

```
         D                 G             A7           D
    A massive live concert would cost millions to stage.
              Bm              E7              Em7          A7
    We could drop the pan flute player and then save on his wage.
                D              G            A7          D
    We could lose all the technicians out there in the wings.
              Bm            E7           Em7         A7
    We could scrap the whole orchestra, including the strings.
            G        A*     A7*   D
    All the musical instruments we could forgo.
           G           A7          D
    Even the piano player could be asked to go.
            G          A7          D          B7* A*    D
    I could do it all digitally at home on my lap-top, now
    Em7      A7         D
    Nothing is real anymore.
```
                        ~**~

Note and Warning to Pianists

Due to popular demand, the piano score for 'Nothing Is Real Anymore' is included overleaf. It can also be downloaded as an MP3 from *the Short Humour Site*.

Parts of this piano arrangement require as many as thirteen simultaneous notes to be played, spanning the whole width of the keyboard. This requires a variation on normal playing technique, as explained below, and should not be attempted by other than fully insured, virtuoso concert pianists. Serious injury, or even death, could result from attempting to play this piece incorrectly.

Between two thirds and three quarters of the notes in most chords can be reached with two human hands. More can be reached by the hands of a large, silverback male lowland gorilla. These creatures, however, have a tendency to rapidly loose interest in the music, often eating the score or smashing the piano to matchwood.

Extenders can be slotted over the fingers of a pianist to extend the range of notes available for each chord. These come in various sizes, and an extender of two feet in length is required on each index finger to successfully play this piece.

In addition, however, shoes and socks should be removed so that toes can be brought into use as required. Some performers have found it more convenient to contort themselves into a position where one leg can be deployed within the piano to directly operate the hammers.

The above techniques should make nearly all bars of this work accessible. For the remainder, it will be necessary to identify an additional convenient bodily protuberance to strike the keys. A lady may wish to use her nose or tongue. An additional option is available to male musicians, although they must ensure that the lid of the piano is securely fixed in the up position.

Piano Score for 'Nothing is Real Anymore'
by Swan Morrison

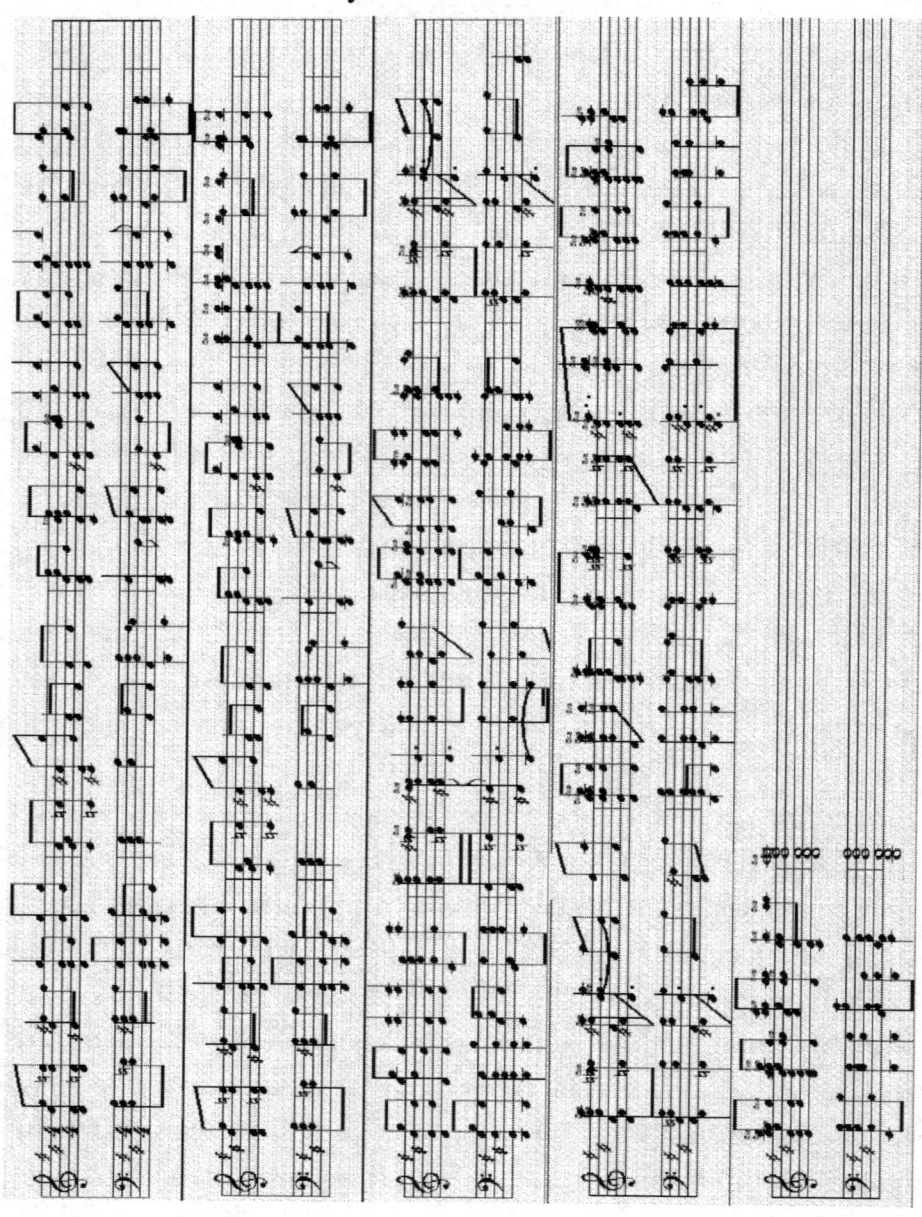

~*~*~*~*~

Also from the Short Humour Site:
http://www.short-humour.org.uk/

***A Man of Few Words by Swan Morrison.

***People of Few Words - Fifty Writers from the Writers' Showcase of the Short Humour Site.

***People of Few Words - Volume 2 - Fifty More Writers from the Writers' Showcase of the Short Humour Site.

All profits from the sale of work by Swan Morrison are currently donated to a UK registered charity supporting people in Africa.

Please visit *the Short Humour Site* to learn more and see how you might help.

~*~*~*~